VALE

W. R. INGE

VALE

BY THE VERY REV.
WILLIAM RALPH INGE, K.C.V.O., D.D.
DEAN OF ST. PAUL'S 1911–1934

LONGMANS, GREEN AND CO.
LONDON · NEW YORK · TORONTO
1934

LONGMANS, GREEN AND CO. LTD
39 PATERNOSTER ROW, LONDON, E.C.4
6 OLD COURT HOUSE STREET, CALCUTTA
52 NICOL ROAD, BOMBAY
36A MOUNT ROAD, MADRAS

LONGMANS, GREEN AND CO.
114 FIFTH AVENUE, NEW YORK
221 EAST 20TH STREET, CHICAGO
88 TREMONT STREET, BOSTON

LONGMANS, GREEN AND CO.
480 UNIVERSITY AVENUE, TORONTO

Printed in Great Britain

VALE

It is, or used to be in my time, the custom for boys who were leaving Eton to write a " Vale " in Latin elegiacs, instead of the regular verse composition which we did every week. Perhaps not many boys had enough Latin at their command to give poetical expression to their love of the school, their sorrow at leaving it, and their hopes or fears on reaching man's estate. But the " Collegers," at any rate, had acquired a facility in the use of that curiously flexible and graceful instrument, the Ovidian couplet, and we wrote in it more easily than in English.

I have now come to the time for a more solemn " Vale," not only to my delightful home at the Deanery, to kind friends, and varied interests, but to active life itself. I think I have said my say and given my message, such as it is ; and it is far wiser to retire before the inevitable decline of one's powers becomes manifest to the outside world. Of course I cannot tell whether I have finished my earthly probation, or whether God will allow me a few peaceful years in retirement, to prepare myself better for the next great change. I shall be quite content either way. Meanwhile, I think I may venture, in this little book, to sum up some of the results of my experience. As I once wrote : " We cannot make a religion for others, and we ought not to let others make a religion for us. Our own religion is what life has taught us. If we can clarify this body of experience, we shall have done what is best worth doing for ourselves, and we shall have to offer to others the best that was in us to give, however small its value may be."

Retrospect for me is a compound of shame and thankfulness. I see too clearly how miserably unworthy I have been of all the blessings which God has given me, and for this reason I have given strict orders that no memoir of me shall be published after my death. (The curiosity of the public about the private lives of men and women is so great that the man with two talents, as well as the man with five, has reason to fear that his imaginary merits may be disclosed, and his frailties dragged from their dread abode to tickle the ears of the groundlings, when he is no longer there to defend himself.) I wish to be remembered, outside my family circle, only by my books, into which I have put what I wanted to say to the public. I have always tried to speak the truth, and to give honest work. There

is nothing intimate about this " Vale " of mine,
except the mention which I have thought right
to make of the nervous troubles in my earlier
life. It reproduces only the pictures which
Memory, that capricious spirit, has preserved,
like peaks, rising mysteriously clear, out of the
mist which has engulfed most of our past lives
and experiences. There is deep wisdom, I
think, in what the Orphic tablets say about the
evil of forgetfulness. The Soul, when it reaches
the other world, is forbidden to approach the
Well of Lethe, and is to draw near to another,
" by the Lake of Memory," and to beseech the
guardian of it, " Lo, I am parched with thirst
and perish. Give me quickly the cool water
from the Lake." There is so much, alas, that
we have no right to forget.

I cannot understand how anyone can wish to
write an autobiography, unless, indeed, he wants
to leave a flattering and by no means honest
self-portrait. How often, when I am awake at
night, I seem to see a procession of grinning
goblins, each saying, " Look at me. I am what
you did and said and thought, and left undone."
Many men, no doubt, take the sage advice of
Goethe. " Above all, no reproaches about
what is past and cannot be altered ! How could
a man live at all if he did not grant absolution

3

every night to himself and all his fellows?"
But there are some offences, especially sins against
the law of love—ingratitude to those who are
no longer alive to witness our repentance—
for which we may hope to be forgiven, but for
which we can hardly forgive ourselves. I do
not advocate brooding over the irreparable.
An educated Jew once said to me, "In our
religion, repentance means, not 'Grieve,' but
'Turn,'" and I think when our Lord spoke
of repentance He meant the same. Julian of
Norwich even says that for the saved soul his or
her past faults are felt "no longer as wounds but
as worships." There is a sense in which the
grace of God may "restore to us the years that the
locust hath eaten." But it is hardly for us "to
grant ourselves absolution." Shame and remorse
for opportunities missed, time worse than wasted,
fine characters and minds not appreciated, are the
right punishment for our faults, and perhaps a
sign of forgiveness. Were not Adam and Eve
forgiven when "their eyes were opened"?

Charles Kingsley, when he was asked whose
character he disliked most, said, "My own."
My feeling is that since I do not exactly dislike
myself, there is nobody else whom I have a right
to dislike. But, as the hundred-and-third Psalm
says, "God knoweth whereof we are made; He

4

remembereth that we are but dust." Faults
which we cannot remember to have been ever
without, which seem to have been part of our
inheritance, will, we may hope, be mercifully
dealt with, if we have tried to overcome them.

The typical ambitious man, I suppose, faces
his prospective biographer with equanimity.
He has kept him in his mind's eye from the first.
Whether he is writing a letter of condolence, or
his first impressions of the Lake of Lucerne, he
thinks subconsciously, " How will this read in my
Life and Letters ? " He decides early that he will
be a judge, or a bishop, or a cabinet minister, and
drills himself always to behave, and if possible
to look, like that kind of person. Habit soon
becomes second nature—and, for that matter,
nature is only first habit. By the time he is a
bishop, it is no effort to him to be dignified,
fatherly, and cautious. By the time he is a judge,
he looks, even in his bath, as wise as a stuffed owl.
By the time he is a cabinet minister, he looks as
if he had been born in a frock-coat, and has
acquired the art of fulminating for an hour
without saying anything at all. Such lives lack
psychological interest, being entirely directed
outwards ; but unquestionably this kind of
honourable ambition inhibits a crowd of tempta-
tions, and produces very useful citizens.

Ambition, said Cardinal Wolsey, caused the fall of the angels—which does not prevent Satan from being the only interesting character in *Paradise Lost*. In practice, I think, ambition has two roots. It is sometimes the diversion of the fortunate, but more often the refuge of the unhappy. Borrow suggests that secret unhappiness is often the goad which leads to worldly success. "Who have been the wise ones, the mighty ones, the conquering ones of the earth? The joyous? I believe it not." One feels rather sorry for those who are so equably balanced that they are good for nothing in particular. But they are pleasant companions, philosophers of the school of Epicurus.

In one of the books which contain a collection of my fugitive essays, I have given some of my early reminiscences. I have described my early home in the North Riding of Yorkshire, far away from the railway and with very few neighbours. No children now have such a good education as we had, for both our parents, who were scholarly, and admirable teachers, gave up a great part of every day to their family, instead of sending them off to school. There are very few parents who have the leisure to do this, and fewer still who have the patience and ability to train their children day by day from the time

6

when they have learned to speak to public school age. There was a great deal of learning by heart, including a considerable part of the New Testament, nearly all the Psalms, and many chapters of Isaiah. There are several chapters of the Bible which I can repeat without a mistake to this day. There was also a great deal of reading aloud. This excellent practice was so much the rule in antiquity (we may remember the story of Philip and the Ethiopian), that Augustine was surprised to find Ambrose reading silently, and supposed that he did it to spare his voice. A good book, especially poetry, should be read aloud. One advantage is that it prevents us from reading too fast. There is also the pleasure of sharing the book with a friend. Since my marriage, my wife and I have read many books together in the early morning.

The isolation of our life at Crayke was not good for us in all ways ; but we never thought it dull. The habit of rushing about from place to place, and of craving for amusements, was unknown to us as to very many of our contemporaries. I do not think that the change has been altogether for the better.

The religious atmosphere in which I was nurtured was not that of my own generation, but that of the early days of the Oxford Movement.

There must be very few now alive who can remember what that atmosphere was. My grandfather, Edward Churton, Archdeacon of Cleveland and Rector of Crayke, had been a friend of Pusey and his contemporaries. He continued to correspond with them, and Copeland, one of the group, was a frequent visitor at the Rectory. Manning came once, after Newman's secession and before his own. This was, of course, long before my birth. I do not think my grandfather liked him. But in spite of occasional intercourse and correspondence with the outer world, the churchmanship of Crayke was purely the Tractarianism of the 'forties. Of all the leaders, Keble was the most kindred spirit. His reverence for the memory of King Charles the Martyr, his intense loyalty to the old Anglican tradition, his admiration for the Nonjurors, his horror of dissent and of every hint of theological liberalism, his ingrained conservatism, his profound unworldliness and simplicity, and his refined, scholarly piety, were all characteristics of my early home. For my father, able scholar as he was, was the humblest and most loyal of men. There was not much difference between the atmosphere of " The Cottage," where we lived, and that of the Rectory.

The High Churchmanship of an old Tractarian

home would hardly be recognizable as such now. There was no ritual ; I do not think my grandfather ever wore a cassock. We were taught to fast in Lent—not, however, by abstaining from meat, but by drinking sugarless tea and eating rice-pudding, which we hated. The verbal inspiration of the Bible was almost as much insisted on as among the Evangelicals, and the Sunday was a slightly mitigated Puritan Sabbath. Theatre-going was not exactly sinful, but in fact we never went there. Novel-reading was allowed, but chiefly the classics, like Walter Scott. New novels, with " yellow backs," were severely frowned upon. Above all, the slightest concession to liberalism in theology was denounced with unqualified indignation. The names of Colenso, Stanley, Jowett, and Arnold were mentioned with horror. " Low Churchmen," as the Evangelicals were called, were spoken of with pitying tolerance, except when they interfered with the Tractarians ; but a " Broad Churchman," we were given to understand, was absolutely outside the pale. The awful fate of Korah, Dathan, and Abiram was impressed upon us in such a way that we should not have been much surprised to see the Methodist minister swallowed up by the earth.

All this makes it easy for me to understand

9

both the deep piety and the fierce bigotry of the Oxford Movement. That the religion of the men who belonged to it was real and deep cannot be questioned, and in their own way they were learned. They read both the Fathers of the Church and the old Anglican divines, but they naturally made no attempt to keep up with what they called German theology. The evolution of the Anglo-Catholic movement has been so rapid, and has displayed so many changes, that some may doubt whether those who showed such enthusiasm in celebrating the centenary of Keble's famous sermon on National Apostasy really represent the mind of those who have been lately called the Oxford Apostles. These pioneers of the movement would certainly have denounced unsparingly the opinions held by many modern High Churchmen.

In order to understand the position of Anglo-Catholicism in the last hundred years, we must bear in mind the changes in the relations of Church and State since the Restoration. The Church of England under the Stuarts was a national institution, the nation on its spiritual side. Even in 1872 Döllinger could write : " No Church is so national, so deeply rooted in popular affection, so bound up with the institutions and manners of the country, or so powerful in its

influence on national character." The bond
between it and the monarchy was indissoluble
in the seventeenth century. The kings ruled
by divine right, and a change of dynasty was a
problem of conscience for every churchman.
Hence the importance of the Nonjuring schism,
and the question of the limits of passive obedience.
Jacobitism was not entirely dead even within
my memory ; my mother, though a loyal subject
of Queen Victoria, was as devoted to the Stuarts
as John Keble. Our Prayer Book, especially
the now discontinued commemorations of the
martyrdom of Charles I, the Restoration of 1660,
and the Gunpowder Plot, show how close the
union of Church and State was all through the
eighteenth century. No doubt the Church
suffered in the same way as the State from the
comfortable security of the national life in that
period. The portraits of the eighteenth-century
bishops in almost every episcopal palace compare
unfavourably with those of their predecessors and
successors. When the eighteenth century spoke
of "enthusiasm," it meant something vulgar,
undignified, and hysterical. But there had been
no coldness or prosaic unspirituality about the
best of the typical Anglicans of an earlier time,
such as Hooker, George Herbert, Andrewes,
Ken, and the greatest of all, William Law, who

hardly seems to belong to the generation when he lived.

The breach between Church and State began with the Liberal movement in politics after the Napoleonic war. It seems to us monstrous that the Tractarians should have been violently excited about the suppression of a few Irish bishoprics, and strange that most of them opposed Catholic emancipation and the first Reform Bill. The bishops, it is true, had been roughly advised to "put their houses in order"; but their houses were very much out of order. Nepotism and jobbery were rampant. The fears of a triumph of Benthamism and irreligion were groundless; the removal by the State of abuses which the Church refused to remove was a friendly act. But the result was that the Tractarian party began to regard the State as an enemy. The sacred character of the monarchy was not easy to believe in when the king was not a picturesque Stuart, but the absurd William IV, with a head like a pine-apple. It was more serious that the Tory ministry and the bishops could not be relied on. So, just as the Nonjurors had broken off from alliance with the State on what for them was a question of conscience, the Tractarians began to talk about the independence of the Church, and to accuse of Erastianism

the old High Churchmen and the new Liberals
—men like Arnold and Stanley—who were true
to the old doctrine that the Church is the nation
on its spiritual side.

Newman's idea of a *via media* snapped in his
hands. But after his secession a new compromise
arose—the churchmanship of the " Good Churchmen," of whom Samuel Wilberforce was the
chief founder. These men raised the standard
of clerical efficiency in the parishes, and en-
couraged, on the whole, a moderate Anglo-
Catholicism, loyal to Anglican traditions and on
friendly terms with the State, which under the
leadership of Gladstone was very well disposed
towards the Church. Parallel to this was a great
increase of what was called " ritualism "—an
emphasis on ceremonial frankly borrowed from
Rome. The Tractarians themselves had regarded
these externals with distrust and contempt.

My own introduction to the new ritualism
came rather late, when my family moved to
Oxford. For a short time I used to attend
Sunday services at St. Barnabas, where I was
attracted by the brightness and spectacular beauty
of the services. But the preaching was wretched,
and the teaching was not really to my taste.

It was about this time that the High Church
party struck out on two new lines. The

Tractarians were mostly high Tories, and they did
not take much interest in what Carlyle called the
condition of England question. The appeal for
social reform had been the special work of one
branch of Broad Churchmen, headed by Kingsley
and Maurice. But by this time a large number of
young Anglo-Catholic priests were working in
the poor parts of our large towns, and had
acquired more sympathy with the political and
social aspirations of their parishioners. They
remembered that the Church in the past had
often come forward as the champion of the poor
and the oppressed. The group of Oxford dons
who had contributed to the volume called *Lux
Mundi* was strongly imbued with political radical-
ism. It was by no means rare to find priests
who avowed themselves socialists. Gore and
Scott Holland were the most prominent movers
in this change of front, which was in no way
inconsistent with Anglo-Catholic principles,
though the new enthusiasm for drastic social
legislation was startling to many old-fashioned
High Churchmen. It must be remembered that
at this time there still existed several abuses
which have since been remedied, so that we
cannot assume that the " Christian Socialists "
of the Victorian age would now join the Labour
party. The earnest priests who revealed the

evils of sweating and overcrowding did good service in awakening the social conscience.

The other new departure, of which Charles Gore made himself the spokesman, would have filled the Tractarians with dismay, and did in fact scandalize Canon Liddon, whose last years were embittered by the fear that his best disciples were breaking away from orthodoxy as he understood it. In my young days, as I have said, there was not much difference between High and Low Churchmen on the subject of biblical inspiration. Perhaps the " days " of creation were not periods of twenty-four hours. Perhaps the author of the Book of Jasher allowed himself some poetical licence. Perhaps the fish that swallowed Jonah was not a whale. This is about as far as the spirit of rationalism was allowed to go. But the authors of *Lux Mundi* were scholars, who saw that the maintenance of the old theory of inspiration had become utterly impossible. They also realized that bibliolatry was not the foundation on which Anglo-Catholicism rested. To abandon these indefensible outworks would strengthen, not weaken, the citadel ; so Gore boldly admitted that if Christ attributed the hundred-and-tenth psalm to David, He was mistaken. Protests were made, but the writers stood their ground. The barriers in the way of free criticism of the inspired books were gradually broken down, at least as regards the Old Testament. More caution was necessary in dealing with the New; and an attempt was made by Gore and others to exempt all historical statements made in the Creeds from adverse criticism. On this point he expressed himself with great vehemence. " There must be no compromise as regards the Creeds. If those who live in an atmosphere of intellectual criticism become incapable of such sincere public profession of belief as the Creed contains, the Church must look to recruit her ministry from classes still capable of a more simple and unhesitating faith." He acted on this declaration with harshness, in dealing with one of his clergy at Birmingham. But he could not keep his party at the point at which he wished to stop; there was no logical justification for putting the Creeds above the Bible, or for treating some articles in them, arbitrarily selected, as more important than others. The High Church party was soon much more Liberal than the old Evangelicals, whose adherence to what the Americans came to call fundamentalism made it difficult for educated men to remain in their ranks.

Another modification of the old Tractarian attitude was coming about insidiously. The original movement rested on a theory of the ministry rather than of the Church. A true Church was one which possessed the "Apostolic Succession," the priestly authority imparted by devolution from the Twelve Apostles to their successors. The sacraments administered by these duly authorized and privileged ministers were "valid"; those of Presbyterian and Nonconformist Churches were not valid. This is the theory of the ministry in which I was brought up. It has never been formally abandoned; it is still strong enough, in an important section of the Anglican Church, to prevent any reunion with the other Reformed Churches on terms which those Churches could accept without abandoning their own traditions and convictions. It is peculiar to Anglicanism. The Roman Church holds that since Anglican bishops have not the intention of ordaining Catholic priests, the continuity has been broken, and Anglican Orders are "entirely null and void." We need not, and we do not, attach any importance to this verdict; but the effect of it is that those who hold the stiff Anglican doctrine of Apostolic Succession virtually divide all other Christians into those who unchurch them and those whom they unchurch. It is even more fatal that the doctrine is historically untenable; the first links in the chain are broken, or rather never existed. The doctrine also belongs to a static theory of the Church. Its title-deeds are nearly two thousand years old, and any defect in them cannot be repaired.

Bishop Gore adhered to this theory to the end. " The various presbyterian and congregationalist organizations, in dispensing with the episcopal succession, violated a fundamental law of the Church's life." " A ministry not episcopally received is invalid." Nevertheless, "God's promise to Judah was that she should remember her ways and be ashamed, when she should receive her sisters Samaria and Sodom " (!)— i.e., the Presbyterians and the Free Churches— back into her fold. But if I am not mistaken, the more thoughtful High Churchmen no longer lay much stress upon it. The more modern tendency is to regard the Church as a real continuation of the Incarnation, the fulfilment of our Lord's promise to be with us all the days, even to the end of the world. The gift of the Holy Spirit is the presence in the world of Christ Himself under another form. Those who value the Church as a divine institution believe that this gift is possessed not only by individuals but by the corporate community. The Church, through its officers, can speak with authority, and may hope for divine guidance. Its sacraments are normally the special channel through which grace is imparted to the individual. It seems to follow, if the Holy Spirit is a dynamic force in the world, that revelation is not stereotyped, but progressive. The Church may learn, and may adapt its teaching to new conditions.

Thus expressed, the dynamic view of revelation as a living Spirit instead of as an unchanged deposit of doctrine would perhaps be accepted with only a few dissentients. But the change from the earlier doctrine preached by the Tractarians is really very great. It makes the test of a true Church no longer external and mechanical, but moral and spiritual. " By their fruits ye shall know them." The possession of " the mind of Christ," not the validity of our title-deeds, becomes the criterion whether we are true to the intention of the divine Head of the Church. A society with the Apostolic Succession may fall away from grace. It may become heretical ; it may become corrupt. And on the other side, when we see a dissentient body, which " followeth not us," exhibiting, so far as we can judge, the fruits of the Spirit, can we dare to say that that body is outside the covenant of grace ? The Tractarians answered this question with a peremptoriness which few Churchmen would now wish to emulate. Many still hesitate to offer the right hand of fellowship to Unitarians, most of whom profess their belief in Christ as our perfect pattern, but not in the formulas of Nicene orthodoxy, and to the Quakers, who have no sacraments. But even in these cases it is generally recognized that all who love the Lord Jesus Christ with sincerity have a right to the name of Christians, which they claim for themselves. The hostility between the Church and Dissent has diminished enormously within my recollection. In my young days, the aloofness of the Church was partly snobbish; the clergyman was supposed to be a gentleman, the dissenting minister was not. This cause of irritation has practically disappeared, and so has the sour animosity against the Church which used to be very common among Nonconformists, some of whom remembered legal disabilities which have now been done away with long ago. It is not likely that anything more than an *amicabilis concordia* can be established, but in scholarship, moral and social reform, and all the many half-secular " causes " in which ministers of religion in this country rightly take an interest, hearty co-operation is not only possible but easy. The hostile forces in our civilization for the most part threaten all forms of Christianity alike, so that wisdom suggests a united front against a common enemy.

The change of which I have just spoken has had an effect on the feelings of Anglicans towards the Church of Rome. As long as the Puritan tradition was alive and vigorous, the Roman Church was condemned for being tawdry, idolatrous, and superstitious. In the vigorous words of a seventeenth-century writer, it is the merit of the Church of England to steer a middle course "between the meretricious gaudiness of the Church of Rome and the squalid sluttery of fanatical conventicles." When the Pope, in a famous allocution, issued about 1865, condemned those who assert that the Roman Pontiff can and ought to reconcile himself with liberalism and modern civilization, he was saying nothing with which the Tractarians would not have heartily concurred. Now, even Anglo-Catholics quote this pronouncement as a proof that the Papacy is reactionary and obscurantist. On the other hand, we no longer look at "idolatry" with Jewish eyes. Even Evangelicals are losing their suspicion of artistic decoration, symbolism, and sacred music as aids in the worship of God. But to repudiate the possibility of any new revelation, any advance in knowledge which may make some part of our tradition untenable, this is indeed an

offence to that spirit of the age which has not
been without influence upon the Anglo-Catholic
party. To put it briefly, the Tractarians were
fiercely anti-Modernist; the very idea of evolution in doctrine was anathema to them. Their
successors to-day have accepted a mass of what
fifty years ago would have been considered
dangerous heresies. Such hostility to new ideas as
still exists proceeds rather from the old-fashioned
High Churchmen than from the Anglo-Catholics.

These concessions to Modernism can be made
without difficulty by those who believe in the
teaching office of the Holy Spirit, immanent in
the Church. Newman was no stranger to the
idea of development, and is sometimes quite
erroneously called the father of Modernism.
A more grotesque attempt has been lately made
to find Modernist sympathies in Keble. Both
would have spurned the imputation with horror.
But some of their successors have found it
possible to combine acceptance of well-established
conclusions in science, criticism, and history with
an unabated attachment to the Catholic faith.
Their motive for these acceptances is one which
some traditionalists find it strangely hard to
understand. Our contemporaries accept the new
science, the new criticism, the new history
because, to the best of their belief, the new ideas

and discoveries happen to be true. Traditionalists often seem to regard this consideration as
irrelevant. For them, the parson is a cheapjack,
paid to sell certain wares. He need not ask
whether they are genuine or not ; but if he does
not cry them up, he is " dishonest." The layman
often agrees with him. " Well," he will say,
" it is not a job I should care for myself ; but if a
man chooses to earn his living as a parson, he
must speak to his brief." This view of the
clerical office is most degrading ; and it is nothing
short of treason to the younger generation, who
will listen with pathetic eagerness to an older
man whom they believe to be speaking from his
heart, though most of them do not want to hear
what " the Bible says," or what " Holy Church
teaches."

The enthusiasm of the Anglo-Catholic party
for social or socialistic reform seems to have
abated somewhat since the deaths of Gore and
Scott Holland. I do not regret this, for it has
been the glory of the Church of England that
there is no Church party in secular politics.
No Church has ever gone into politics without
coming out badly smirched. Individual Churchmen may be, and ought to be, if they are well-
informed, interested in schemes of social legislation ; but to advocate a sloppy socialism under

the name of " Christian politics and economics "
is, in my opinion, an impertinence. These are
questions on which high-minded Christians
notoriously differ, and we have no right to
assume that our political friends alone have the
mind of Christ.

There has been, I think, an increasing tendency
to make the Holy Communion the centre of
Church life, and to encourage attendance at this
service without actually communicating. In
many churches " reservation " is practised, and
this kind of devotion soon becomes popular.
This marks a still further departure from Anglican
tradition, and those who dislike it are tempted to
talk of " magic " and " materialism," where
those who value it see only a helpful symbolism.
Another change, which is apparent to those who
read the parish magazines of typical " extreme "
churches, is the concentration of interest upon
the services of the Church. It is a new kind of
parochialism, or rather congregationalism, since
many of the worshippers come from a distance.
It is difficult to believe that this is a healthy sign.

I have allowed myself this digression, because
the changes in Anglo-Catholicism within my
own recollection have naturally made a great
impression upon me. The party has, on the
whole, retained the loyalty of its older members,

who were brought up on very different lines, and this has made the enforcement of any kind of discipline extremely difficult. The most "advanced" members of the party are really not Anglicans at all, and their parishioners have a very legitimate grievance if the services in the only church which they can attend without inconvenience are changed from Anglican to Roman against their wishes; but if the bishops try to stop these irregularities, they arouse the opposition of many who do not wish to practise them themselves. The policy of deliberate law-breaking has been only too successful.

In the short reminiscences to which I have already referred, I have spoken of the immense debt, which I owe to both my parents. I deeply regret that in my much busier life I have not been able to discharge the obligation in the only proper way, by doing as much for my children. My father would not leave Crayke while my grandfather lived. In 1874 he was given the benefice of Alrewas, near Lichfield, by Bishop Selwyn, and so returned to the county with which my family have been connected for more than three centuries. After six years of work in that parish, during which he restored the church mainly out of his own pocket, Lord Salisbury made him Provost of the College at Oxford of

which he had been a Scholar and Fellow. The
house and grounds at Worcester College are
beautiful, and this remained our happy home till
my father died in 1903. He had an opportunity
of higher preferment, for Lord Salisbury offered
him the bishopric of Salisbury, to which, when
he declined it, John Wordsworth was appointed.
My father refused by return of post. " I could
only say that I have not the qualifications," was
his own statement when some years later, he
revealed the secret. It is possible that he was
right ; he was a slow worker and not an impres-
sive preacher ; but most men would have been
tempted by such an offer. There are few, if
any, more attractive dioceses in England than
Salisbury, which includes the two charming
counties of Wiltshire and Dorset. My mother
lived on at Oxford after his death, and died
during the War at the age of eighty-three.

There is one subject on which I should have
much preferred to keep silence. A natural
pride and reticence make it odious to divulge
humiliating weaknesses. But my one object
in this little book is to give the benefit of my
experience to those who may read it, and I believe
I have had many fellow-sufferers. Of my three
chief friends and rivals at Eton, two, after distinguished and outwardly happy careers, ended

by finding the torment of mental depression more than flesh and blood could bear. The third, Arthur Christopher Benson, has himself recorded the attacks of melancholia which darkened several years of his later life, when he was Master of Magdalene College, Cambridge. In his case the cloud lifted before his death. I probably suffered more than any of them in boyhood and youth, but the trouble left me in early middle life. My miseries, which were mainly hypochondriacal, began before I was seven years old, so that it is not necessary to call in the unpleasant Doctor Freud. But I could say with Tennyson, " From the time of my marriage the peace of God descended upon my life " ; and I have no doubt that when a man suffers from these troubles, and the *acedia* to which they lead, the blessed realization that he loves and is loved is the best of all remedies.

These miseries, whatever form they take, are a kind of rationalized psychalgia. The victim knows that he is wretched, and does not know why. So he fastens upon something which, if it were true, would account for his unhappiness. Sometimes, like the poet Cowper, a man of blameless and amiable character, he fancies that he has committed the unpardonable sin, and breaks into horrible lamentations :

" Damned below Judas, more abhorred than he was
Who for a few pence sold his holy Master,
Twice betrayed Jesus me the last delinquent
Deems the profanest."

Sometimes he half believes that he is financially
ruined. Many misers, I suspect, begin in this
way, before the passion for accumulation finally
masters them. Others persuade themselves that
they are despised and hated by everybody.
Others half believe that they are deformed, or
victims of maladies unknown to science. In every
case the cause is the same, deep-seated nervous
depression, which they are unable to account for.

From the religious point of view, these are the
most mysterious of all dispensations, since they
make even belief in God (as in poor Cowper's
case), a source of misery and despair. They
seem to be merely crippling, and destructive of
the " love, joy, and peace " which, as St. Paul
says, are the fruits of the Spirit. When I think
of my three friends, all men of the highest
character as well as of great ability, I cannot
understand how God allowed them to be so
afflicted.

No doubt, overwork at school and at the
university was a contributory cause with my
friends and myself. We were, I am afraid, very
jealous of each other, and we worked fiercely,

sitting up till the small hours in defiance of rules. As for the results, after we came into competition with other young men at Cambridge, are they not written in the Cambridge University Calendar? We swept the board of all the classical distinctions, but a price had to be paid. I was walking with Hugh Macnaghten in the Eton playing-fields a short time before the end, and finding him very dejected I told him more about my own early troubles than I had ever revealed to anyone else, and also how completely they had disappeared. He only said, " The fact is, my dear Inge, you and I both worked much too hard here and at Cambridge. I have never recovered from it." But my troubles began much earlier than the struggle for the Newcastle Scholarship.

Parents ought to look out for signs of un-accountable depression in their boys. (I suppose girls sometimes suffer in the same way, but I think less frequently.) My parents did not understand me at all. My father, who had the placid and healthy temperament of a family of athletes, could only say, " Remember good Bishop Hacket's motto—Serve God and be cheerful." Alas! How could I be, with a legion of devils waiting for me in my unoccupied moments?

I believe the right method is to force the boy
—it is very difficult—to make a clean breast of
his troubles and put them into words. When
dragged into the light of day, the delusions seem
manifestly absurd. The boy will probably be
driven to say, " Well, I suppose I do not really
quite believe these things about myself, but I am
as miserable as if they were all true." That is the
first step to recovery ; the boy will henceforth
realize that his troubles have no external justification. Nothing helped me more than the dis-
covery that if I woke up in the night, I could
tell the time within an hour by the state of my
spirits. A mental temperature of below zero
meant that it was between three and five !

A wise man has said that we are never really
so happy or so unhappy as we imagine we are.
Nervous depression is not continuous, and I
have no doubt that through most of my waking
hours I was either fairly happy or too much
occupied to think whether I was happy or not.
But the torture of the hours when the black fit
was on me has stamped itself indelibly on my
memory.

After only three months at a preparatory
school, I stood for a scholarship at Eton, and
was elected second on the list, the first being
Herbert Tatham, an unambitious man of

extraordinary ability, who afterwards became a master at Eton, and lost his life in the Alps. It was an unusually strong year; but, alas, only two of the eleven who entered college in September 1874 are still alive. My luck attended me in my father's choice of a tutor. After trying two of the younger masters, whose lists were full, he put me under Thackeray, a cousin of the novelist and formerly a Fellow of Lincoln College, Oxford. Thackeray had the same enthusiasm for the classics which my father had imbibed from the famous Dr. Kennedy at Shrewsbury. He was a first-rate teacher, the best tutor at Eton for boys who wished to work, and perhaps the worst for those who did not. I owed him a great deal.

In 1879 I went up to Cambridge as a scholar of King's. My undergraduate career is mainly a record of scholarships and prizes, though I sometimes played for my college at cricket, and was very fond of the game. I think the work that I enjoyed most was when I was reading for the ancient history section of the Classical Tripos, Part II. It amuses me to remember that I obtained leave from the college authorities to absent myself from the elaborate choral services on Sunday afternoons in King's Chapel, on the understanding that I went to a parochial service in the evening.   I little knew what the fates had in store for me.

I did not think of being ordained till I had been an Eton master for three years. I received deacon's orders from Bishop King of Lincoln, on my fellowship of King's, which by an anomaly is still in the diocese of Lincoln, and not of Ely. I was then twenty-eight, and I was for some time so uncertain of my vocation that I did not proceed to priest's orders till four years later. I left Eton to become a Fellow and tutor of Hertford College, Oxford, at the end of 1888, just at the time when I was ordained deacon.

Oxford and Cambridge are more like each other than either of them is like any other place in the world; but there are differences. I became interested in philosophy as soon as I migrated to Oxford, though it was not my business to teach it; and I tried to find a sound intellectual basis for my religious belief. It was in this way that I came to study Christian mysticism.

What is the seat of authority in religion? Historically, there have been four—an institution, a book, the inner light, and human reason. Most Christians agree that all four contribute something, but they differ widely as to their relative importance. Hooker, a very typical Anglican divine, says : " What Scripture doth plainly deliver, to that the first place both of credit and obedience is due ; the next whereunto is whatsoever any man can necessarily conclude by force of reason ; after these, the voice of the Church succeedeth." The primacy here given to Scripture is plainly the doctrine of the Prayer Book, as the occasional offices show. " The Bible," said Chillingworth, much too strongly, " is the religion of Protestants." Archbishop Laud declares that all four are necessary ; the work of the Holy Ghost in us is not the same as the force of reason, to which he assigns the negative office of confuting error.

It is clear that the Church and the Bible are both external authorities ; if either of them is given the first place, reason and illumination are no longer independent. During the wars of religion, after the beginning of the Reformation, each side was driven by the necessities of controversy to appeal to an external and infallible authority. Theology in both camps was hardened and coarsened ; even the mysticism of the Counter-Reformation—for example in John of the Cross—was harsh and stern. But when the stress of conflict was relaxed, illumination and reason, mysticism and philosophy, came again into their own. I have tried to show, in some of my later books, how what I have called the Platonic tradition has quite as good a claim to its place in Christianity as the slogans of militant Catholics and Protestants. From St. Paul and St. John to the Alexandrians, and from them to Scotus Erigena and Eckhart and the Cambridge Platonists and Bishop Westcott, the chain is unbroken. This school finds its authority partly in Christian philosophy, which is Platonic rather than Aristotelian, and partly in what modern writers call religious experience. Mysticism based on a foundation of reason—this summary statement may serve to indicate the general character of Christianized Platonism.

It became clear to me, as soon as I began to think seriously about the foundations of belief, that the centre of gravity in religion has shifted, in our day, from authority to experience. To ascribe infallibility to the pronouncements of the institutional Church seems almost monstrous. Nothing can be more fantastic than the Tractarian theory that the General Councils were infallibly guided, but that the gift of infallibility went into abeyance when the Church was divided, like an old English peerage when there is more than one daughter but no son. Plenary authority, according to this theory, belongs to a council which can never meet. It is much as if no Act of

Parliament were valid which had not been voted at a joint session of the House of Commons and the American Congress. Fanatical loyalty to an ecclesiastical organization, which gives the Roman Church the driving force of a standing army, is the temper, not of Christ, but of the Jerusalem hierarchy who crucified Him. And yet, like all other perversions, it is the corruption of something good. For the Church began as a brotherhood, not as a collection of individuals with identical beliefs. Aubrey Moore, who was abreast of the science of his time, found that in physics and biology the idea of organism was prevailing over that of atomism, and claimed that the same tendency was reviving the idea of the Church as a divine society, in which " men become members of an organic whole by sharing in a common life." At that time " socialism " and " individualism " were favourite catchwords in political controversy, and the *Lux Mundi* writers proclaimed that they had no sympathy with " individualism." The historical study of religions was revealing that, in the words of Troeltsch, " the essence of all religion is not dogma and idea, but cultus and communion, the living intercourse with the Deity, an intercourse of the entire community." The American philosopher, Royce, wrote a book to prove that

the essence of Christianity is "loyalty to the
beloved community," though he left it quite
vague where, if anywhere, the beloved community
is to be found.   Lastly, the politico-philosophical
doctrine of the " general will," supposed to be
wiser and better and more authoritative than the
mere resultant of the opinions of the voters,
though in politics it is little more than a stick
with which to beat minorities, gives a sort of
mystical value to the pronouncements of the
Church.

There has thus been a revival of institutionalism, in accordance with one tendency, at least,
of the spirit of the age.   It is impossible to find
any sanction for a militant political Church in the
New Testament.   But the Catholic Modernists
argue that this development was inevitable ;
it was forced by circumstances upon the Church,
which had to consolidate itself against persecution
from without and against disruptive movements
within.   If Christ meant His Church to survive,
they say, He could not have disapproved of the
only policy which could ensure its survival.
This, however, is a bad defence of an institution
which claims to be divine.   Force and fraud are
not the weapons of the Holy Spirit.   As I wrote
in 1914, " What the Latin Church preserved was
not the religion of Christ, which lived on by its

inherent indestructibility, but parts of the Aristotelian and Platonic philosophies, distorted and petrified by scholasticism, a vast quantity of purely pagan superstition, and the *arcana imperii* of Roman Caesarism. The normal end of scholasticism is a mummified philosophy of authority, in which there are no problems to solve, but a great many dead pundits to consult. The normal end of a policy which exploits the superstitions of the peasant is a desperate warfare against education. The normal end of Roman imperialism is a sultanate like that of Diocletian."

It is plain that I could not attach myself to the rigid institutionalists, whether Roman or Anglican. It was equally impossible for me to ally myself with those who held that " the Bible is the religion of Protestants." The Biblical writers themselves never claimed verbal inerrancy. It was the Church which drew up the Canon, deciding which books were to be considered inspired. Some books, both of the Old and New Testaments, have unquestionably been assigned to wrong authors and to wrong dates. The traditional views about the Bible have, in fact, been so riddled by criticism that they can no longer be held honestly by an educated man. It was this, more than anything else, which led to the downfall of the old Evangelical party.

The new Evangelicals are still hampered by their old traditions, though they are freeing themselves by degrees, as they discover that theirs is not really the religion of a book, but the religion of the Spirit. But the old theory, which treated the Old and New Testaments as one book, has made our services far more Jewish than they need be. We who have come to love the familiar words can hardly realize how strange and how meaning- less much in our services must appear to those who have not been brought up as Churchmen.

I had therefore no choice but to study religious philosophy and the writings of the mystics. I soon found that here I was on firm ground. I have never myself had what are usually called mystical experiences. But in truth the typical mystical experience is just prayer. Anyone who has really prayed, and felt that his prayers are heard, knows what mysticism means. The higher stages of the inward ascent are for the saints who have given up all to win the pearl of great price. We who have neither surrendered so much nor gained such a victory over our lower selves cannot expect to reach them. But it by no means follows that the testimony of the saints is not valid except for themselves. We do not argue in this way about experts in other branches of human endeavour. We are thankful

to learn from them and to believe what they tell
us. The uniformity of the testimony given by
the mystics is most remarkable, and can be
reasonably explained only by believing that they
have actually seen what they tell us that they have
seen. I was convinced very early, and I have
never wavered in my conviction, that this testimony of the saints and mystics has far greater
evidential value than is usually supposed, and
that it may properly take the place of those
traditional " evidences " which for one reason or
another have lost their cogency. Of course
the contemplatives can testify only to spiritual
things. They can tell us nothing about past
or future events. But they can testify to what
we most wish to know—that the eternal things,
which are not seen, are real, and that we can, if
we prepare ourselves properly, ascend in heart
and mind to the " place " (we can hardly help
using this word) whither our Saviour Christ is
gone before.

Mysticism stands or falls with a belief about
human nature which is not held by all. St.
Paul clearly held it. He divides our nature into
body, soul, and spirit. The soul-life is the stage
in which we mostly live, when we are not
" walking after the flesh," which is a living
death. But there is a higher stage, that of spirit,

which is in a sense super-personal, since the
Spirit of God, who dwells in us, is not part of
ourselves. The soul is thus the wanderer of the
metaphysical world. It has its own natural
sphere, but it may rise above it or fall below it.
And *we can only see what we are.* " Such as men
themselves are, such will God (and the world)
appear to them to be." These words of one of
the Cambridge Platonists explain the theory of
knowledge on which the philosophy of mysticism
rests. " The natural (or psychical) man cannot
know the things of the Spirit of God, because
they are spiritually discerned." In other words,
knowledge of self and knowledge of God must
proceed *pari passu.* As we climb higher up the
hill of the Lord, the landscape opens out before
us. So, " if any man willeth to do his will, he
shall know of the doctrine." It is impossible to
say where, in the spiritual life, the human will
leaves off and divine grace begins. It is, as von
Hügel says, the mysterious paradox which
pervades all true life, that the human soul is
active in proportion to God's action within it.
A man is never so truly and intensely himself as
when he is most possessed by God.

The mystics have described for us the normal
stages of the pilgrim's progress. They use the
words purification, illumination, and union, the

last being the ideal goal rather than the highest stage of the ascent. They do not mean to suggest that the lower stage comes to an end when the higher begins. We never cease to need the discipline of purification ; the eyes of our understanding are progressively enlightened ; and on the other side, we could not take even the first step if the Holy Spirit were not already an inmate of our souls. Clement of Alexandria has a slightly different chart. The first step, he says, is from heathenism or unbelief to faith. Faith is " a voluntary assent," a kind of anticipation of what we afterwards come to know. Then faith gradually passes into knowledge. Our experiment becomes an experience. And knowledge in its turn passes into love, which unites the knower and the known. He who has reached this stage, he adds, is perhaps " equal to the angels."

Proclus the Neoplatonist has the penetrating remark that the lowest and highest grades in the spiritual ascent are simple, the middle complex. Faith, which Frederick Myers defines as the resolution to stand or fall by the noblest hypothesis, begins as a simple act of the soul, an act of trust, a venture. But as our experience widens, the richness and complexity of the outer and inner world are opened out before us.

41

All kinds of problems distract us ; the wisdom, goodness, and beauty of God are manifested to us in bewildering multiplicity. Those, however who are called to the " unitive life " find these varied colours harmonized and almost absorbed in " the white radiance of eternity." Clement anticipates Proclus, when he says that as " knowledge passes into love," it recovers, on a higher plane, the simplicity of its first act of faith.

My first published work on the subject of mysticism was my Bampton Lectures, given at Oxford in 1899, when I was in my fortieth year. I tried to cover, to some extent, the whole ground of Christian mysticism in the eight lectures, which were a good deal expanded for publication. I had to include in one volume the philosophy of mysticism, the mysticism of the New Testament, the ascetics of the cloister, and the nature-mystics like Wordsworth. I was breaking new ground, for the only book on the subject which was much read in England was Vaughan's *Hours with the Mystics* ; and this, though it has real merits, does not treat with sufficient reverence the highest quest to which the human spirit can devote itself. My book was well-timed, for the public was ready to realize the importance of the study. It became for a time the standard work on the subject, and it still has a steady sale. But I did not wish to pursue my studies of the mystics of the cloister, and was glad to surrender this side of the subject to Miss Evelyn Underhill, whose excellent books have introduced many thousands to the treasures of Catholic mystical literature in the Middle Ages. The Quakers, who have always kept up the tradition of devotional meditation, have produced fine studies of the history of mysticism, and valuable devotional books based on their experience of the inner light, or testimony of the Holy Spirit in the hearts of men. Even greater attention was aroused by works on religious psychology, of which William James' brilliant *Varieties of Religious Experience* is the best known. From my point of view, these psychological studies are not altogether satisfactory. The psychologist, while he confines himself to his own subject, is interested only in states of consciousness as such. The question of the objective truth and value of what the mystic regards as divine revelations does not concern him. This is very different from the attitude of the mystics themselves, whose whole interest is concentrated in the truth of what God has revealed to them. They are often deeply troubled by the suspicion that their visions may be the work of their imagination, or even delusions emanating from the enemy of souls. The psychologist can hardly ignore (as he does ignore) the question whether revelations are what those who receive them believe them to be, or whether they are merely subjective, often hallucinatory, impressions, without seeming to prejudge the case against the belief that they are more than subjective. There is then no criterion by which genuine mystical experience can be distinguished from the morbid hysterical visions from which ascetics in particular often suffer. And there is a tendency, both in James' book and in others of the same kind, to give too much space to unhealthy psychical manifestations, ignoring the fact that the typical mystic is not a visionary, and is perfectly sane.

The study of so-called mystical phenomena—illusions of sight, hearing, touch, and smell—is very interesting to the psychologist, but to me it is only repellent. I was attracted to the subject of mysticism by the conviction that those who have devoted their whole lives to the pursuit of holiness, " without which no man may see the Lord," must have something more to tell us about the high places of the spiritual life than ordinary men and women can know, and it was distressing to find out that their overstrained nerves sometimes took their revenge. It seemed to me that these delusions were partly caused by a too complete withdrawal from a natural healthy life in society, and by a too exclusive cultivation of the emotional faculties. Those mystics who were also philosophers—and there is a noble series of philosophic mystics—were almost free from these aberrations, and were not inferior to the cloistered contemplatives in spiritual insight. I determined therefore to make a special study of them.

The mystical tradition in Christian thought may also be described as the Platonic tradition. Plato was a many-sided man, and some of his interests, such as mathematics and political philosophy, were taken up by thinkers who did not belong to his school. It is as a prophet and mystic and champion of the immortality of the soul, that his influence has been strongest and most permanent. In my Hulsean Lectures at Cambridge I showed that until the beginning of the Dark Ages Christian Platonism was the dominant type of religious philosophy; that even before the Renaissance it was revived in the speculations of John Scotus Erigena and in the scholastic Neoplatonism of Eckhart; and that since the new birth of learning it has inspired many of the deepest religious thinkers, especially in our own country. I have often tried to arouse interest in that most interesting group, the Cambridge Platonists of the seventeenth century. The writings of Benjamin Whichcote, best known in the very acute and stimulating aphorisms collected from his sermons, a book still to be found in many old libraries, and the sermons of John Smith, whose early death deprived the Church of a very noble spiritual guide, are among the most admirable contributions to English theology and homiletics. The chain is almost unbroken from them to Coleridge, Wordsworth (especially in the *Prelude*), Erskine of Linlathen, and Westcott. William Law, after he began to study Böhme, is a shining light in the prosaic and unmystical eighteenth century.

But I soon found that the greatest of all mystical philosophers was the Egyptian Plotinus, who taught at Rome in the middle of the third century after Christ. I began to work upon him before I left Oxford, but from 1905 onwards my studies were much interrupted by changes in my abode and in my professional work. During the years when I was Vicar of All Saints', Ennismore Gardens, I had very little time to give to the philosophy of religion. I resumed my task when I became Lady Margaret Professor of Divinity at Cambridge in 1907, and finished it, slowly, at St. Paul's. My book, which I intended to be my *magnum opus*, was almost ready when I received an invitation to give the Gifford Lectures at St. Andrews. This obliged me to recast the whole book, which now had to be arranged in twenty lectures. I have the pleasantest recollections of my visits to St. Andrews in 1917 and 1918. There is a peculiar charm about that little university town with its ruined cathedral and other monuments of the Middle Ages. Andrew Lang confessed that St. Andrews had almost stolen his heart away from Oxford. My lectures were given in unusual circumstances, for nearly all the students were serving their country in the Great War. My audience consisted chiefly of the professors and of ladies. My second course coincided with the Armistice, and there was a general fraternization on the following Sunday, when I preached in the famous Kirk over which Dr. Boyd used to preside, and the Episcopalian bishop sat under me. I have twice visited St. Andrews since, once to receive an honorary degree, and once to preach the university sermon.

So much of the honey of Plotinus was carried off to the Christian hive by Augustine, and by the mystical writer whom the Church knew as Dionysius the Areopagite (he was really a disciple of Proclus in the fifth century) that he almost belongs to the evolution of Christian philosophy. In fact, after Porphyry the best part of Neoplatonism was Christian ; for the later members of the school were more and more attracted by theurgy and magic, against which this philosophy is insufficiently protected, in consequence of its theory of a hidden sympathy running through the whole of nature. St. Augustine was converted from Manichean dualism, and from the materialistic conception of Spirit which we find even in the Christian Stoic Tertullian, by his study of the Platonists, and especially of Plotinus, who taught him the meaning of " God is Spirit." He says in the *Confessions* that he found almost all that he wanted in these philosophers, *except* the Incarnation. " The Word was made flesh—that I found not among them." " God so loved the world "—*sic Deus dilexit mundum*—the words are inscribed above the altar in St. Paul's. How man should love God, and learn to know Him—this Plotinus teaches us very well. But the object of devotion, for the Platonist, is super-personal. That God should love us, and " come down " to raise us up, as we could not raise ourselves—this is not so easily fitted into the scheme of Platonic philosophy, though it is not incompatible with it. The human soul can rise into the spiritual world, for thence it came and thither it can return ; but the downward movement, to which the world in space and time owes its existence, is left unexplained, except by the theory that the Divine nature, which is essentially creative, must express itself, so far as may be, in every possible grade of being. No philosophy, as far as I know, can really explain *why* there is a world. We must just accept it. The higher part of the soul, so Plotinus taught, can suffer no contamination. A bad man may " lose his soul," certainly ; but not the soul which would have been his if he had not been a bad man. There is no room for " spiritual wickedness in the heavenlies " in this system ; and therefore the darkest kind of evil— the " defilement of the *spirit*," in St. Paul's words, is hardly recognized, and the need of an Incarnation is not felt. This defect was so strongly realized by Augustine that he soon accepted the full Christian revelation, but he continued, at any rate in his earlier and better-known writings, to be a Platonist. His influence on the whole course of Catholic theology, even to our day, can hardly be overestimated.

What can a Christian learn from Plotinus ? These among other lessons. The Godhead, as He is in Himself, apart from the creation, "dwelleth in the light which no man can approach unto." He is the Unity underlying and transcending all plurality, all differentiation. That there is such a Unity is implied by the Unity-in-duality of the spiritual world, where Spirit and the objects which Spirit contemplates correspond entirely and reciprocally imply each other, but still remain distinguished as subject and object. According to this philosophy, no duality can be quite ultimate ; there must be a unity behind it. This metaphysical argument is reinforced by the highest flight of mystical experience, when the spirit, rapt into a trance, seems for a time to cease to be itself, and to have a momentary glimpse of the supreme source and goal of all being. Plotinus himself thought that he had had this experience on a very few occasions ; his successors hardly expected to have it at all ; but ecstasy remained part of the possible experience of the Christian mystics, and it clearly represents an actual feature of the contemplative life. Whether it really reinforces the metaphysical doctrine of the " One beyond existence," may be doubted. It is not an essential part of mysticism, as a practical system, since it rarely falls within the experience even of the greatest saints ; far too much emphasis has been laid upon it by critics of Neoplatonism and mysticism. But it is the apex of the metaphysical pyramid.

The heaven of the Platonist is not the " One beyond existence," nor does Plotinus often use the word God of the " first principle." The heaven of the Platonist is the eternal, timeless, and spaceless world in which the God who reveals Himself to man dwells. His essential attributes, as known to us, are Goodness, Truth, and Beauty. It follows that the soul can " become Spirit " and enter into eternal life by the diligent practice of the Good, by the disinterested quest of the True, and by admiration and love of the Beautiful, which to a Greek includes " beautiful " actions and characters. To see God in these His attributes, and these attributes in Him, is to know God and become like Him.

For at every stage in the ascent of the hill of the Lord the law holds that only like can know like. We can only know what is like ourselves ; what we know and love, that we are. Our rank in the scale of being depends on what we really care about ; where our treasure is, there will our heart (Plotinus would say our " soul ") be also. This is the sufficient answer to those who have found what they call " intellectualism " in the Platonists. The instrument through which we acquire divine knowledge is not the logic-chopping faculty. The Greeks never confused νοῦς and διάνοια. It is the whole man, unified in the service of the highest quest ; it is the intellect, will, and affections all acting together, that practise faith, which the Epistle to the Hebrews defines as " seeing the invisible." As Julian of Norwich says : " Our faith cometh of the natural love of the soul, and of the clear light of our reason, and of the steadfast mind which we have of God in our first making." This gift is not ours to start with. Spiritual things can only be spiritually discerned. He who wishes to ascend in heart and mind to the realm where God dwells must put himself under a lifelong discipline (not of harsh asceticism ; the Platonist lives plainly but does not maltreat his body) ; and he must keep every avenue open by which beams from the world of light may reach him.

All things, Plotinus would have us believe, are naturally attracted upwards to the sphere next above them ; as Proclus puts it in a striking phrase, " all things pray, except the Supreme." Earthly blessings are made light of ; earthly sorrows are dismissed even too lightly by this philosophy. For in all Greek thought there is the desire to make oneself invulnerable. The Christian also may speak of " our light affliction, which is but for a moment " ; but the Christian does not try to be invulnerable ; however heroic he may be in bearing his own troubles, those of others—his family, his friends, his country, and other nations too, move him deeply. Benevolence does not for him, as it did for the Stoics, take the place of sympathy.

These things, and much more, I found in Plotinus. I was again fortunate in my choice of a subject; many other scholars were ready to take it up. It is now generally recognized by those whose opinions carry weight that the great thinker of the third century is one of the foremost names in the history of philosophy, and certainly one of the most powerful defenders of a spiritual view of life. Von Hügel, it is true, tries to distinguish between Plotinus the saintly seeker after holiness, and Plotinus the metaphysician, whose system, he thinks, banishes God from the world, and bids us approach Him by emptying our minds of all content. But he has been misled by his authorities, who use the word " God," where Plotinus speaks of the One, the Absolute. I do not think that von Hügel has studied Plotinus deeply at first hand. The spiritual world (κόσμος νοητός) is full of rich contents; no mutilation of the personality can lead a man there; and we are tartly warned that " to try to rise above Spirit (νοῦς) is to fall outside it." The real limitations of Neoplatonism are those which I have mentioned as having been discerned by Augustine.

I wrote several smaller books while I was still at work on Plotinus. *Personal Idealism and Mysticism*, which I delivered as lectures in America on the Paddock Foundation, is partly polemical, provoked by a book of essays called *Personal Idealism*, by some friends of mine at Oxford. The group to which these philosophers belonged seemed to me to have a needless distrust of the intellectual processes as a means of arriving at divine truth, leading to the sceptical conclusion that since absolute truth, if there is such a thing, is unattainable by us, we may believe whatever seems to help us. I also thought that by over-estimating the separateness of individual personality, they neglected the doctrine of the mystical union with the glorified Christ, which seemed to me at once the most blessed and the most verifiable part of the Christian revelation. Further, their doctrine of time compelled them to interpret eternal life as, quite literally, survival in the future, which lands us in great difficulties when we ask where and when a framework for this future existence can be found. My friend Rashdall, who, though no pragmatist, was associated with this group, was impelled by his combative disposition always to seize a poker by the hot end, and in consequence had a reputation for heresy which he certainly did not deserve.

He thought it very hard that a Platonist may steal a horse when an Aristotelian may not look in at the stable window, and when he was asked whether he approved of my appointment as Dean, he replied, "Why not? Inge is a Buddhist." Bernard Shaw was nearer the mark when he called me a Quaker.

In 1904, while I was still a tutor at Oxford, I published a volume of university and other sermons, under the title of *Faith and Knowledge*. I have printed only two other collections of sermons, *All Saints' Sermons*, when I left my West End living, and the little book called *Personal Religion and the Life of Devotion*. A sermon is a kind of speech, not a kind of essay, and a good parochial sermon seldom reads well. University sermons are of a rather different kind. The volume *Faith and Knowledge* contained an Oxford university sermon on Liberal Catholicism, which attracted a good deal of attention and criticism. My attitude towards Catholicism is, perhaps, somewhat unusual, and is certainly very different from that of " Modernists " generally. These latter make a *bête noire* of St. Thomas Aquinas. They accuse the schoolmen of " intellectualism," by which they mean a theology based on concepts capable of clear definition. The logic of the schoolmen, they admit, is beyond reproach, but they juggle with counters which are out of relation to reality. Realities are fluid, and refuse to be reduced to static concepts. Living faith does not depend on dialectic; it is a matter of will and feeling rather than of intellect; truth in this region is pragmatic rather than metaphysical. The idea of evolution, unfamiliar in the Middle Ages, now dominates all our thought. Theology, like everything else, must grow and change.

Newman saw the strength of this position as a justification of later accretions in Catholicism. He was able to show that the germs of many later developments are to be found in the primitive Church, which has grown without any breach of historical continuity. Newman would have shrunk with indignation from the conclusions of Modernism; but it was felt in the Church of his adoption that he had opened the door to a dangerous mode of apologetic. Shortly before I preached this sermon, the Abbé Loisy, a brilliant critic, and at that time in intention a loyal son of the Church, had given a more modern turn to Newman's argument by bringing it into connection with anti-intellectualist philosophy and with something like American pragmatism. He did not stand alone. Blondel, Le Roy, and Laberthonnière, belonged to the same school; and there were able Modernists in Italy. Loisy draws a sharp distinction between what is true for faith and what is true for science. He pours scorn on German Liberal Protestantism as an attempt to dress up Jesus of Nazareth, in defiance of history, as a modern man, a morally perfect Being who "has for us the value of God." The Church, says Loisy, need no more reproduce the forms of the Galilean Gospel than a man of fifty need resemble a new-born child. "When we want to assure ourselves of the identity of an individual, we do not try to squeeze him into his cradle." The development of primitive Christianity into Catholicism was a natural growth.

To this last argument I replied that external continuity is not disputed, and proves nothing. It would prove nothing even if there were no other Churches, with as good a right to exist as the Roman. The necessity of some of the accommodations to pagan superstition and to the exigencies of power-politics has not been demonstrated. Christ Himself rejected the temptation, " All these things will I give thee if thou wilt fall down and worship me." "Necessity, the tyrant's plea," can hardly be adduced to justify such concessions in a divine society. A Church must prove its moral and spiritual, not merely its external, descent from the life and teaching of its Founder. " We cannot," I said, " recognize this identification pre-eminently in the Church of Rome."

But though the history of the Roman Church as a political institution, especially since the Reformation, fills me with a repugnance which, as I know, many of my friends think excessive, I am very far from following the Modernists in their revolt against Catholic philosophy. The philosophy of Modernism, in its repudiation of Platonism, repels me as much as in its virtual repudiation of the Jesus of the Gospels. Jesus of Nazareth, according to Loisy, was a peasant " of limited intelligence," who went about telling people to prepare for a tremendous cataclysm, which never occurred. But this, he thinks, does not matter ; for historical researches tend only to prove and represent facts, which cannot be in contradiction with any dogma, precisely because they are facts. We find the same kind of apologetic in George Tyrrell, who strangely supposed that the Jesuits could accept as a defence of orthodoxy an argument which cuts off the tree from its roots. We acknowledge, said Loisy, *comme deux Christs*—one, the peasant of limited intelligence, the other, an organization with a very dubious record, which demands

" loyal submission " to a series of fact-like dogmas which are not really facts at all. I returned
to the charge in some later essays. Loisy's
last book, *La Naissance de Christianisme* (1934)
must convince even those who criticized my
sermon, that I saw better than they did where he
wished to lead us. This book is the most brilliant and most dangerous attack upon Christianity,
as a historical religion, that I ever read.
The Pope's declaration that Modernism is " a
compendium of all the heresies " misses the
mark only because none of the old heretics
thought of representing Christ as an ineffectual
kind of Mahdi, an agitator like Theudas. My
attitude towards the official philosophy of
Catholicism is explained in my latest book,
God and the Astronomers, in which I acknowledge
a debt to the Neo-Thomists.

Two other short books of mine belong to the
same period—*Truth and Falsehood in Religion*
(1906), and *Faith and its Psychology* (1909). Both
were given in lectures at Cambridge. I have
the pleasure of knowing that the former course
of lectures decided a man, who has since risen
to high distinction in the Church, to take Holy
Orders. My book on *Faith* had only a moderate
sale, but I think it is the best of my theological
works ; there is hardly anything in it that I

should now wish to alter. I also gave, in 1906, a course of lectures at St. Margaret's, Westminster, published under the title of *Studies of English Mystics*. These lectures were popular in form, adapted to the taste of an educated congregation with no special knowledge of the subject. In 1909 I contributed to *Cambridge Biblical Essays* an essay on the theology of the Fourth Gospel. And in 1911 I was asked to take the annual Quiet Day for public schoolmasters and dons. The four addresses which I gave on this occasion were published under the title of *Speculum Animae*. I took great pains with them, and I think they have helped many people. The little book has gone through several editions, and still has a sale.

Earlier than these was the volume of essays called *Contentio Veritatis*, published in 1902. This was a kind of manifesto by a group of Oxford tutors who were interested in Liberal theology. The book had a large immediate sale, but has not had a permanent influence comparable to that of *Lux Mundi*, or the later *Foundations*. The other contributors were Hastings Rashdall, afterwards Dean of Carlisle ; H. L. Wild, afterwards Bishop of Newcastle ; C. F. Burney, afterwards a professor at Oxford ; W. C. Allen, afterwards Archdeacon of Manchester, and A. J. Carlyle, afterwards Canon of Worcester. Herbert Williams, now Bishop of Carlisle, promised an essay, but was unable to finish it in time. I wrote two essays, one on the Person of Christ, the other on the Sacraments. Rashdall's essay is rationalistic, idealist, and largely Kantian—a very able argument from this side. My discussion about the Person of Christ is on the lines of the Logos-Christology and the Fourth Gospel. All historical revelation is a manifestation of the eternal counsels of God, rather than an irruption of the supernatural into the natural order. In applying this principle I was a little more cautious and reserved than in some of my later writings. My essay on the Sacraments did not please the Anglo-Catholics. Rudimentary sacraments, I said, are found in primitive religions in connection with sacrifices. The ideas which they express are (1) the establishment of guest-friendship with the god; (2) acquisition of divine qualities by sacramentally eating the gifts of the god or the flesh of his totem-animal; (3) atonement for sin by the sacrifice of the totem-animal, which represents both the god and his worshippers. The idea of sacrifice is realized when priest, victim, deity and worshippers are made *one*. In the Greek mysteries or sacraments the boon conferred was immortality or deification. The sacrament of admission consisted chiefly of ceremonial washing : the sacrament of membership, of a common meal. The Christian sacraments are thus the simplest and most universal of all sacramental rites. The elements in the Jewish sacramental worship which our Lord wished to exclude were bloody sacrifices and sacerdotalism. Among the accretions which gathered round the primitive Christian sacraments, chiefly from the Greek mysteries, were (1) symbolism, the sacraments as mystical symbols of spiritual truths ; (2) secrecy ; (3) materialization of the doctrine of sacramental grace ; (4) ritualism and spectacular worship ; (5) the idea of the sacraments as " the medicine of immortality." These are not all unhealthy developments. The attempt to dispense with symbols in religion is a mistake; the relation of the outward to the inward is real, but the question of causation had better be set aside. The doctrine of special channels of grace is easily abused. We must not make God the upholder of unjust privilege, or presume to decide who is, or is not, " outside the covenant of grace." The dignity of the priestly calling is prophetic rather than sacerdotal. In the Eucharist it is an eternal act that we represent, not a temporal act that we repeat. The great sacraments are intended to teach us that all life is, in various degrees, sacred and sacramental. In particular, the Eucharist should help us to realize the deep mystery of our relation to our fellow-men, which perfect love alone can solve.

I was a fellow and tutor of Hertford College for fifteen years, and I enjoyed my quiet life in College rooms. But the time came, as it comes to many college dons, when I began to wish for a home of my own ; and my interests were gradually detached from the linguistic study of the classics, which it was my business to teach, in favour of the broader questions of philosophy and theology. The old-fashioned enthusiasm for the classics is declining, especially at Oxford. Latin and Greek composition is becoming an elegant accomplishment rather than the finest test of a liberal education. More and more I felt that a purely classical training was only propae-deutic to the study of higher subjects. This view is assumed by the Oxford Honours course, and in the Cambridge Classical Tripos, which is now divided into two parts.

I therefore had no hesitation when the year 1904 brought the great change in my life. My friend Canon Henson, now Bishop of Durham and then patron of the parishes carved out of St. Margaret's, Westminster, offered me the living of All Saints, Ennismore Gardens, vacant

by the appointment of Ravenscroft Stewart to
the archdeaconry of Bristol. At the same time
I became engaged to Mary Catharine Spooner,
elder daughter of the Archdeacon of Maidstone,
niece of the Warden of New College, and grand-
daughter of Bishop Harvey Goodwin of Carlisle.
Thus began the greatest of my earthly blessings,
and a much happier chapter in my life. We were
married in May 1905, in Canterbury Cathedral,
by Archbishop Davidson, a cousin by marriage
of the Spooners. Our first home was at 34
Rutland Gate, in a quiet little square with no
through traffic, and close to Hyde Park. The
parish was aristocratic rather than smart, and
most of my congregation were middle-aged or
elderly, since the district was favoured by
retired business or professional men.

It was entirely new work for me, and I had
everything to learn. But though the golden age
of the West End incumbents was already coming
to an end, I kept my congregation together, and
rather characteristically (for I have always been
unnecessarily careful about money) piled up a
large balance on the parish funds, of which my
successor reaped the benefit. I took great pains
with my sermons, which in the absence of the
usual parochial organizations were the most
important part of my work.

I am glad to have seen something of London before the Great War, which has made such drastic changes in the way of living among the richer classes. There was still an army of men-servants in the parish, and the dinners, especially among the newly rich, tended to be long and sumptuous. Class distinctions were more marked than they are now, and I think the ladies had fewer interests. My congregation contained three of His Majesty's judges, and several other very able men and women. This made the preaching rather difficult, as there were also many old-fashioned people who did not want strong meat. Our parishioners were very kind to us, and I learned a great deal that I did not know before.

It was a brief episode, for in less than three years I heard from Cambridge that my friends wished me to stand for the Lady Margaret Professorship. This Chair is the oldest in the University, and has been held by several eminent men. When I was elected, I was invited to become a professorial Fellow of Jesus College —my third College. I have now the unusual honour of being an honorary Fellow of three colleges, King's and Jesus at Cambridge, and Hertford at Oxford. The Master and Fellows of Jesus were a very friendly society, and welcomed me most kindly. The college itself is one of the most beautiful at either University.

We took a very pleasant house, called Brook House, in Trumpington Street, and for the first time in my life I had the luxury of a garden. No position could be more favourable for a scholar than that which I then held. The professor may choose his own subjects to lecture upon, though he has to remember that his audience consists chiefly of young men who are intending to be clergymen. This was my one disappointment, for though in each year there is a small sprinkling of good scholars reading for the Theological Tripos, the majority, I found, required more elementary teaching than my classical pupils at Oxford, who were all honours men. I did a little independent work with a few of the abler students. My leisure for private study was almost unlimited, since I gave only a few lectures each week in term-time, and had half the year to myself, during the vacations. Three of my five children were born at Cambridge, the eldest was born at Rutland Gate, the youngest at the Deanery of St. Paul's.

I was very busy writing, preaching, and lecturing in London and elsewhere, all the time when I was a Professor. I suppose my mind was then at its best. When I read these old

66

books of mine, I am a little dismayed to find how few new ideas have come to me since, except, indeed, in two fields which I had not then explored—the religious and philosophical implications of recent advances in natural science, and the criticism of Christian ethics from the side of scientific humanism. During the last twenty years, these subjects have taken the foremost place in the public mind, and are now the battle-ground on which the defence of Christianity against its opponents must be fought out.

I had no thought of another uprooting, and looked forward to the cloistered life of a scholar in congenial surroundings. It never entered my head that I was likely to be thought of for promotion in the Church. It was therefore a staggering surprise when, in 1911, Mr. Asquith, who was then Prime Minister, wrote to say that he had nominated me to the Crown for the Deanery of St. Paul's. I was much disposed to decline, knowing that no power on earth could turn me into an ecclesiastic, and being rather afraid of what I had been told of the tone of the Chapter at that time. But I heard from Downing Street that my friends had exerted themselves to procure my appointment, and that if I refused it would be a great disappointment to all who wished Liberal churchmanship to be represented in London. I was also reminded that by tradition the Deanery of St. Paul's is the most literary appointment in the Church of England, and that the wish of the Prime Minister was that I should try to revive the scholarly prestige of the office which had been held by Milman, Mansel, and Church, not to speak of such great names in the past as Colet, Donne, and Tillotson. A man ought to have some very good reason for refusing an appointment offered in such a way, and I had no good reason except that I was very happy where I was, and that I was terribly bored by long musical services. I therefore accepted after a few days' consideration.

I never regretted my decision after the first few months, which were not made very pleasant for me. By an arrangement as unusual as it is undesirable, the retiring Dean was allowed to occupy the Deanery house during his lifetime. This made it very difficult for me to do my work properly. I took rooms in an hotel at Bloomsbury, and my wife remained in our house at Cambridge. It was also a shock, when I talked to the Archdeacon of London about one or two things which I hoped to do, to hear the answer, " As long as Canons X and Y are both here, you are not going to be allowed to do anything." Thirdly, a few weeks after I began

my work, an incident occurred which made me
open my eyes very wide, and showed me what an
unfamiliar variety of the human species it was
my fate to have to deal with. I quote from my
diary for Sunday, June 18, 1911. " A number of
colonial troops were present at the morning
service, and they asked that the organ should
play a verse of the national anthem while they
marched out after the sermon. The Archdeacon
of London, who was in residence, gave his
consent. On hearing this, the senior Minor
Canon rushed into the vestry, where our guest,
the Dean of Gloucester, was robing, and in a
voice trembling with excitement announced that
the Minor Canons would walk out of church if
this was done. In order to avoid the awful
scandal of an insult to the King in St. Paul's,
the Archdeacon revoked his consent, with my
approval." These young gentlemen were not
communists, and of course they had no responsi-
bility for the conduct of the services, which is in
the hands of the " Ordinary," that is to say, the
Dean and Chapter. They had, it seems, some
cryptic objection to that hymn, or perhaps any
hymn, being played at that point of the service.

As regards the second incident, the warning
that I should not be allowed to do anything, it
must be remembered that by statute the Dean of

St. Paul's has no independent power. He is very like the Head of a college at Oxford or Cambridge, in those colleges where the Head is not in charge of any department. His main duty to the Cathedral—of course he is expected to lead an active life outside the Cathedral—is to exercise a general supervision, to help to make the machine run smoothly, and, if he can afford it, to keep open house. I had to eat humble pie occasionally, and I was disappointed not to receive the friendly coaching in my duties which I needed and expected. But the routine administrative work was done efficiently by others, better than I could have done it myself; and by accepting what a masterful man would have found a somewhat humiliating position I avoided friction with my colleagues. I had really no choice in the matter.

Besides, there was not very much that needed doing. Dean Gregory and his colleagues had put everything in excellent order, and we have had a splendid staff of loyal and efficient workers in every department. I have never known a great machine run so smoothly. Our relations with each other were, I think, good, by the not very high standard of Cathedral Chapters, which have a bad name for quarrelling. Archbishop Davidson once paid me a very high compliment, which I felt that I did not deserve, on my success in keeping such " a difficult team " together. The credit was not mine. I think the main secret was that though we did not all belong to the same school of Churchmanship, we were agreed that the Cathedral services must represent, not the predilections of any party in the Church, but Prayer Book or central Churchmanship, so that no loyal Anglican who comes to worship in St. Paul's will find anything to distress or disturb him. It has not always been quite easy to keep this balance true, but the difficulties have not come from the Chapter.

I had one, and probably two opportunities of returning to academical work at Oxford. In the first case, the Principalship of Hertford, a much better appointment was made. I did not wish to move. If I had twice accepted important positions in London, and twice given them up to take refuge in academic work, the world would have smiled. And I soon made a very full life for myself in London. I became president of several societies. The Religious Thought Society I helped to found. It did good work for about twelve years, during which we had some admirable lectures from several distinguished men, including Baron von Hügel. But it languished after the War, and at last we allowed it to

71

disappear. The Clergy Home Mission Union is an Evangelical society which meets once a month. The papers read at the conferences are often very interesting. I also succeeded Dean Rashdall as president of the Modern Churchmen's Union. This society has branches in many parts of the country, and a very well edited organ, *The Modern Churchman*, for which Dr. Major of Ripon Hall is responsible. When the society was founded, heresy hunts were not uncommon, and it was thought that those who were dissatisfied, in one way or another, with the traditional apologetics might combine for mutual protection against episcopal persecution. But now, it seems to me, there is no longer much need for these measures of defence. The bishops are quite willing to give Liberal churchmen as much latitude as they can reasonably claim. A clergyman has no right to cause unnecessary distress to old-fashioned believers. Most Liberal churchmen think that miracles cannot be proved in such a way as to carry conviction to agnostics, and, what is more important, that if they could be so established, they do not prove what the Christian really wishes to believe. But they would not have entered the ministry of the Church if they were not convinced that belief in the divinity of Christ can be founded on a securer basis. It is for them to build up the faith of others on the foundation which they themselves have found sufficient; and this can be done without attacking the traditional arguments round which the faith of many sincere Christians has twined itself. A Church never formally admits that it has been in the wrong. Obsolete beliefs are allowed to drop off quietly, as we have seen in such examples as the Mosaic cosmogony and the notion that the world is soon coming to an end. Further adaptations to modern knowledge are in progress; some heavy burdens, which are not part of the burden of the Cross, are being lifted from men's shoulders. This is the work of men who in their lifetime endured to be called heretics; and though our society is no longer combative, it is, I believe, doing valuable work. The annual conferences, which are published in the *Modern Churchman*, always contain some good papers. I am not myself an extreme "Modernist," for I have, as I have said, a great admiration for the old Catholic philosophy of religion, of which St. Thomas Aquinas is the most learned exponent. One practical difficulty in our society is that the majority of the members are strong Protestants, and that Liberal Catholicism tends to favour that sharp separation between truths of faith and truths of fact with which I have already expressed my disagreement. But there is a growing school of Liberal High Anglicans who need the sympathy and support which we ought to be willing to give them. With the Liberal Evangelicals our relations are most friendly. They have moved a long way from the " Low Churchmen " of my early recollections. I think, indeed, that in this school lies the best hope for the future of Anglicanism. A devout Christian may be a Liberal Protestant or a Liberal Catholic ; he can hardly be a Liberal without any qualification.

Among my other interests have been the Tavistock Clinic, now called the Institute of Medical Psychology, for treating difficult psychical troubles ; the Council of Malvern College ; the London Library ; and the National Portrait Gallery, of which I am one of the trustees.

I have given a great deal of time and attention to the study of eugenics. I have always been much interested in vital statistics ; and my friendship with that grand old man, Sir Francis Galton, brought me into closer relation with the science which owes to him its name and its first inspiration. I have been a member of the council of the Eugenics Society from the first. It is curious to remember that the Society was then glad to find a dignitary of the Church who was proud to be one of their number. There is still a good deal of prejudice against eugenics, but we have made considerable headway. There is an intelligible antipathy between those who think that social reform consists only in improving the environment, and those who see that nature is even more important than nurture. Schemes of education can only be profitable if the material to which they are applied is sound. We have also, unfortunately, to accept the settled antagonism of the Roman Catholic Church, which will pass no coins that do not bear the stamp of its own mint. There is not much to hope from politicians, who only reflect that the unborn have no votes. It is discouraging to find that those who are proclaiming a crusade against half the ills that afflict mankind are still regarded in some quarters as cranks who wish to interfere with the right of every man and woman to choose his or her own mate.

Karl Pearson, who, I think, is himself a socialist, says : " Our working classes need more than ever some other guidance than that of the politician and journalist; neither of these will lead them to see beyond the horizon of class-interest, or enable them to look upon the nation as an ever-changing organization, susceptible of advance or decay as it obeys or disobeys natural laws." It is this guidance that our Society tries to supply ; and only those who have studied the subject know what misery, and what racial deterioration, are caused by allowing *laissez faire* and ignorant humanitarianism to go on unchecked. When natural selection is forbidden to operate, rational selection must take its place, or we shall have none but a C_3 population.

It seems to me strange that Christians should not be eugenists. Christianity aims at saving the soul—the personality, the nature of man, not his environment. In direct opposition to Marxian socialism, we are taught that from within, out of the heart of man, comes all that can exalt or defile him. For the Christian, as for the eugenist, the test of the welfare of a country is the quality of the men and women whom it turns out. Quality is everything, quantity is nothing. Of course we must not look in the Gospels for anticipations of Galton and Mendel. But our Lord gives us some admirable eugenic precepts. " Do men gather grapes of thorns, or figs of thistles ? A corrupt tree cannot bring forth good fruit, neither can a good tree bring forth evil fruit. Every tree which bringeth not forth good fruit is hewn down and cast into the fire." History shows that dysgenic selection has ruined civilizations. Nature has a short and sharp way of punishing her rebels. " I am not in the habit

76

of talking," Plotinus makes her say. And yet she is willing to teach us if we are willing to learn. The science of eugenics is a young one, and very much remains to be discovered. The more we know about the laws which govern inheritance, the more complex they appear to be. This is a good reason for not agitating for legislation before the facts on which it is to be based are established beyond cavil. But in truth much is already known for certain. We know that much mental defect, disease, vice and crime, might be prevented if obviously undesirable parents could be prevented from adding to the population. We know also what injury is being done by the present policy of taxing out of existence those families which have proved that they possess the qualities which society has hitherto thought deserving of honour. Perhaps we are not all agreed on what qualities we should choose to breed for in our eugenic State ; but there can be no difference of opinion as to the kind of people whom we do not want.

My love of vital statistics has led me to make a thorough investigation of the population question. Probably the most important fact of history in our time has been not the Great War, or social upheavals, but the decline in the birth-rate, which began simultaneously in several

European countries about 1878, and has proceeded steadily ever since. The only exceptions
of importance in a movement which is almost
universal are in Egypt, Palestine, India, Japan,
and the Slav countries, where the conditions are
more Asiatic than European. In Great Britain the
decline has been from 36·3 per thousand in 1876,
to 14·4 in 1933. We have now a lower birth-rate
than any country in the world, except Sweden,
though post-War Germany and Austria have
shrunk from a higher figure to one only slightly
above our own. The births in England, in
proportion to the population, are only about
two-fifths of what they were fifty-five years ago.
For good or evil, it is a momentous change.

Population has always been restricted. No
nation could maintain the natural rate of increase
unless it found itself in a half-empty country.
In the past, the chief agents have been war,
famine, pestilence, abortion, and infanticide. But
the problem has become much more urgent
owing to improvements in sanitation and medical
science. Statistics are easily obtainable. Not to
repeat those which I have given in my other
books, I quote from a paper by two American
experts, dated December 1932. (The duration of
life is nearly the same in the United States and in
England.) In 1800 the expectation of life at

birth for both sexes taken together was about
30 years; in 1880 about 42 years; in 1930 it
was 59·48 for white males, 62·74 for white
females. The writers, using the figures for
New Zealand as the most healthy country in the
world, think that before long an average duration of life of 69 years is not impossible. I
should myself put the probable limit at 65 years
for the two sexes taken together. It is quite
obvious that a birth-rate of 35 could not be
maintained in these altered conditions, least of all
in an overcrowded country like England and
Wales, where the population is 750 to the square
mile. When to this is added the partial loss of
our foreign trade, to which alone we owed the
possibility of the phenomenal increase in the
nineteenth century, it will be plain even to the
most prejudiced that something had to be done
to check further increase.

We are told, truly in a sense, that the globe as
a whole is not overpopulated. The population
is very badly distributed. Compare our 750
to the square mile, or the similar figures in the
small State of Rhode Island, with the three per
square mile for Canada, two for Australia, one for
Nevada. Large parts of these countries are no
doubt either uninhabitable or uninviting for
white men, but the main reason for their sparse

population is their remoteness. Even now, when migration is so much easier than it used to be, there are large fertile tracts in South America which are empty because they are so difficult to reach. I quite admit that much might be done by systematic State colonization, and I have urged again and again that this should be tried; but the obstacles are enormous. We no longer breed good colonists. The urban masses look to the State for everything, and do not wish to lose their share of the rates and taxes by leaving the country. The United States and the Dominions shut their doors against immigrants. The new countries, which in the last century were our great safety-valve, are so no longer. Nor would it be possible to dump an unemployed miner or cotton-spinner on an unimproved farm. All these facts have convinced every unprejudiced observer that the fall in the birth-rate has been absolutely necessary. The command " Be fruitful and multiply," which is said to have been issued when the world contained only two human beings, is inapplicable now that it has to support nearly two thousand millions.

There is no other subject in which public opinion has changed so rapidly and completely as on the morality of birth-control. I can remember the time when the subject was taboo, when Bradlaugh, who advocated it, was called " the unsavoury member for Northampton," and was prevented from taking his seat in Parliament (nominally, no doubt, on the excuse that he was an unbeliever), and when anyone who owned to being a " Malthusian " was suspected of being an immoral person. Now, birth-control clinics are supported by a long list of titled ladies, and by some of the leaders in the great professions. I believe I was the first clergyman to face obloquy by urging that the question ought to be discussed as freely as any other social and economic problem ; now, several well-known ecclesiastics openly support the restriction of families. That the taboo was enforced mainly by intimidation, is shown by the fact—very regrettable on eugenic grounds—that the lowest birth-rates are those of the clergy, doctors, and teachers, the three professions from whom denunciations of the practice were most frequently heard. I find, by consulting *Who's Who*, that, of the forty diocesan bishops, one has five children, two others four each, the remaining thirty-seven only twenty-eight among them.

It must soon be admitted by all, except those for whom discussion is precluded by the supposed obligation not to dispute Catholic authority, that the morality of restricting the family depends on the motive, and that the motive is often good. When my advice is asked by a young couple, I say, " Let two children be born, and afterwards do what you think best for them and for your-selves." As I have had five children myself, I cannot be accused of advocating what has been rather absurdly called race-suicide.

I quite realize that some of the methods employed seem to many to offend against St. Paul's injunction to keep our bodily organs " in sanctification and honour." These matters must be left to the taste and conscience of each married couple. There is also an instinctive feeling that this may be only the beginning of a complete revolution in the relations of the sexes. Those who have read Aldous Huxley's powerful but repulsive book, *Brave New World*, will understand what I mean. Already, it is said, many unmarried girls are less careful of their virginity than they used to be. This is a real danger, which should make us sympathetic towards those who still offer a futile resistance in the service of a cause already lost. There is also some danger that the movement may go too far. It operates very dysgenically, for the only high birth-rates now are among the slum dwellers and the feeble-minded. And on the basis of a stationary population a rate of 14·4 is not enough to prevent an actual though slow decline in numbers. Christopher Dawson, who as a Roman Catholic condemns the practice, gives us a harrowing picture of England and Scotland overrun by Irish, the United States by Mexicans and negroes, France by Italians (who, however, are not undesirable citizens) and Senegalese. To which the answer is that these intruders should be kept out.

My growing interest in these and other aspects of sociology caused me to be asked to give several lectures to scientific bodies. Some of these, with the Romanes Lecture at Oxford, and the Rede Lecture at Cambridge, were published in two volumes of collected essays, to which I gave the not very appropriate title of *Outspoken Essays*—for they contained no startling audacities. The nucleus of these volumes was a series of articles which I wrote for the *Quarterly Review* and *Edinburgh Review*. In their original form they did not attract much attention ; but the two volumes of collected essays had a very large sale, nearly 70,000 copies, I think. A third volume, under a less provocative title, *The Church in the World*, was less popular. These little books contain most of what I have had to say to the public on subjects other than theology and philosophy. The second volume opens with a " Confessio Fidei," in which I tried to explain and justify my religious convictions, and a course of lectures on " The State, Visible and Invisible." I think I may claim that most of my predictions, which at the time some thought too lugubrious, were fulfilled in the unhappy years which have followed the War.

My Gifford Lectures on Plotinus—my most solid contribution to philosophy—were very well received, and went into a third edition. But the subject is far from being exhausted ; the text of Plotinus needs much more attention than I could give to it, and the philosophy of Proclus, the greatest of the Neoplatonists after Plotinus, was almost untouched in this country till Professor Dodds took it up.

In 1923 we had to bear a great sorrow in the death of our younger daughter, Margaret Paula, a very dear child, who in a short life of eleven years gave proof of extraordinary beauty of character. To commemorate her I added to the little book of sermons already mentioned a biographical notice, a portrait, and a Latin poem. This has been the most popular of all my books. I rejoice to know that it has helped to comfort thousands of parents who have had to bear the same grief. Many of the letters which I received were inexpressibly touching, and illustrated the words of the medieval visionary, Julian of

Norwich, " To me was shown no higher stature than childhood."

Soon after I came back to London, by an inexplicable accident which in the case of a shy scholar was almost ludicrous, I found myself very much in the limelight. The newspapers decided that I was " good copy," and reported at length, often very unfairly, whatever I said or did. For a time I was in danger of becoming a kind of Aunt Sally for journalists of the baser sort. More than once I was obliged to decline to speak in public, unless reporters were excluded. This petty persecution was brought to an end partly by the publication of *Outspoken Essays*, and partly by the vigorous protests of men who were as far as possible from agreeing with my opinions, such as Mr. Bernard Shaw and Mr. Nevinson. But I remained " good copy." I was soon approached by newspapers with a large circulation, and asked to become a regular contributor. The remuneration was so lavish that if I had chosen to bargain through an agent, instead of always accepting the sums first offered, and if I had continued to write a few years longer, I should have made my fortune. I had no wish to do this ; but I valued the opportunity of making my opinions known to the general public. The editors gave me a perfectly free hand, and

provided me with a much wider pulpit than I
could have had in any other way. I was able
to present my views on religion, politics, literature, and other subjects to countless readers,
many of whom knew nothing of my more serious
writings. It was also, I confess, some satisfaction
to know that I could make a large income in the
open market, and acquire a facility in a lighter
style than I had practised before. So I wrote
once a week for several years. Many of these
fugitive essays were collected in two volumes,
which had a good sale.

There is a natural jealousy among professional
journalists against those whom they regard as
interlopers ; but in a democratic age there is no
reason why those who have the ear of the public
should not preach the truths in which they believe
to the largest possible audience. The clergy do
this every Sunday from the pulpit, and the press
has now to a large extent taken the place of the
pulpit and platform as a popular educator. I
was of course frequently attacked ; and my
decided views on politics and religion brought
me into conflict with those who did not agree
with me. In politics these were mainly socialists,
a few of whom represented me as an enemy of
the working man. This was really hardly fair.

We are in the middle of a very interesting

experiment. For the first time in history we are trying to extend the best gifts of civilization to the whole nation instead of confining them to a privileged class. This is obviously an experiment well worth trying. Apart from considerations of justice, a civilization which rests on a narrow base is always precarious. It may be uprooted by a violent revolt of the sub-man, as we have seen in Russia. Or it may die down with its custodians. For in history nothing fails like success. A ruling class always rules itself out. For instance, the old Roman families were practically extinct in the third century after Christ. Paganism perished partly because there were no more hereditary pagans. Western civilization for about fifteen hundred years was based upon feudalism, which began when the towns which the Romans founded everywhere fell into decay. The only class which could keep its head above water were the large landowners, who lived on the produce of their estates, and gave protection to many who fled from the violence of barbarian raiders and the rapacity of the tax-collector. This system, after a very long innings, outlived its usefulness, and was moribund even before the Great War and its *sequelae* destroyed it. Now the industrial civilization which supplanted it is itself on its trial.

87

It may be true that a country without any rich men can hardly be a civilized country ; but many who are not socialists think that industrialism has had the effect of giving an unreasonable amount of wealth to a few persons. In the Bible, both in the Old and the New Testaments, we are taught that a very moderate income— " neither poverty nor riches "—is more wholesome for its possessor than a large fortune.

But though this is true, and I do not think I have ever denied it, we must regretfully admit that power is always abused. " Let it be remembered," says Sir John Fortescue, " that the governing class always provides for itself out of the public purse ; that it is doing so at this moment ; and that the cost under the new governing class is about a thousand times as great as under the old." The masses at Rome were not elevated by an unlimited provision of *panem et circenses*. And therefore I do not like to see the clergy, who were monarchists under a strong monarchy, and oligarchs under the oligarchy, tumbling over each other in their eagerness to become court chaplains to King Demos. The black-coated advocates of spoliation are not a nice lot. " I take what I want," said Frederick the Great ; " I can always find pedants to prove my rights."

On the whole, however, I have had very little to complain of from the Labour Party. My relations with the *Daily Herald* are very friendly. I cannot quite say the same about *la bonne presse*. The manners of Giant Pope have not improved since the time of Bunyan—possibly I have given the giant some provocation! and one prominent Anglican Church newspaper has not treated me much better. It is difficult to estimate the amount of injury which the press can do to a public man, but I doubt if it is very great. Sometimes after reading some venomous attack I have been tempted to say, " This is the manure which makes my reputation grow." But undoubtedly many clergymen and others have been taught to regard me as a foolish and objectionable person.

For many years I have been a monthly contributor to the *Church of England Newspaper*, edited by Mr. Herbert Upward, who has proved that a Church paper may live and flourish without party politics, religious or secular, without distortion or misrepresentation of the truth, and without any personal malice or discourtesy.

To return to my more solid literary labours. I was asked to contribute to a volume called *Contemporary British Philosophy*, in which the best-known among our philosophers gave a résumé of their philosophical position, with a short auto-biographical sketch to show what influences had been brought to bear upon them. I also wrote, in *The Legacy of Greece*, an essay on Greek religious thought, and its influence upon Christianity. I contributed to two volumes of scientific essays, called *Science, Religion, and Reality* and *Evolution*. I was, in fact, becoming more interested in the problems of science in relation to religion, metaphysics and ethics than in the psychology of mysticism, on which I had said what I had to say.

A new departure was the volume on *England* which I was asked to write for Messrs. Benn's "Modern World" Series. This was a very interesting, but very difficult, task, since the plan of the whole series was "a survey of historical forces." The book was well received, but it was unlucky that I wrote in the year of the general strike, when I was full of indignation at a concerted attempt to wreck our whole social order. This bitter feeling was reflected in several passages in the book; and like many others at that time, I did not realize the full gravity of unemployment. In the fifth edition, published in 1933, I rewrote part of the book, and tried to maintain a more judicial attitude towards social and political problems. My position was and is that no revolution, in the ordinary sense, is necessary or probable. We may keep our liberties, unless a revolutionary movement gathers such strength as to compel society to mobilize its forces in self-defence. The problem of unemployment can be solved only by reducing the home population; and I expressed my preference for systematic colonization as against a further reduction in the birthrate. When this adjustment is made (I fear it will be many years before it can be made) I believe that applied science will make it possible for the whole population to live in comfort, with somewhat shorter hours of work than now prevail. The people will then, I hope, use their leisure in all kinds of arts and crafts, compensating for the necessary monotony of their paid work by enjoyable and productive hobbies. I emphasized strongly that the demon of class-hatred and class-war must be exorcised if our country is to recover and prosper.

I wrote also a little book on *Protestantism*, for Messrs. Benn's sixpenny series.

But all who are awake to the tendencies of our time must realize that the storm-centre of the conflict between Christianity and its opponents is now the problem of Christian Ethics. In the last century, even those men of science who were most hostile to or contemptuous of dogmatic

Christianity had for the most part no quarrel with Christian morality. The leading scientists in Queen Victoria's reign were men of strict and exemplary lives ; they did not quarrel even with the rather puritanical code of morals which was supported by public opinion during the life-time of the old Queen. But the younger generation has no reverence for tradition, and wishes to emancipate itself from all prohibitions which cannot be shown to have a rational foundation. The codes which the experience of civilized humanity has thought precious enough to be put under supernatural sanction are now subjected to new tests, and if they cannot pass them they are cast aside. We naturally wish to know what the new standards are. But this question is not easy to answer. The chief criterion is utilitarian or hedonistic ; we wish to be as happy as possible, and to see others happy. Sin is made almost co-extensive with anti-social behaviour. But besides this, there is a code of scientific ethics, with which I have already expressed my sympathy—that which bids us aim at the improvement of the race, and also recognizes a moral duty to show humanity to animals, and not to spoil the beautiful things in the world.

What ought the attitude of a Christian to be towards this new morality ? This is the subject of my *Christian Ethics and Modern Problems*, published in 1930. It contains my latest opinions on many burning questions. I am much more sympathetic towards scientific humanism than many Christian writers on ethics. For example, I have fully admitted that the original Gospel leaves us with no clear guidance or encouragement in what for many men and women to-day is the purest and most disinterested of their aspirations —the desire to help in making human life in this world a better thing in the future than it is now. " The rapture of the forward view " was spoilt for the first Christians and long afterwards, by their strange delusion that they lived in " the last time." This means that we have to admit a number of new duties which are not recognized by traditional casuistry. In my attitude towards birth-control, euthanasia, and other test-questions, I am, with some reservations, on the side of the new morality against the old. At the same time I believe that no morality based on secularism can be satisfactory. As I wrote, "It is through the divine life in men, the Christ in us, that ethics belong to the eternal or spiritual world, and that moral conduct becomes as it were the sacrament, the outward and visible sign, of faith, hope and love directed to a Being who in His nature sits above the conflict between right and wrong. What is relative and subjective in morality is thus anchored to absolute truth and goodness." " Christianity is a divine life, not a divine science."

There has been, as I have said, a revolt against some parts of New Testament morality ; the imperfections of Old Testament morality have long been recognized. I tried in my book to deal with these questions in a temper of strict candour. There is and must be a conflict between secularist and religious ethics ; we must recognize at once that our standards are based on principles which are not accepted by all moralists. It is not our business to please everybody, not even all good people.

We must not assert that the Church has always been supernaturally protected from error. In no age has the Church escaped from powerful reactions emanating from secular conditions. The persecutions hardened the temper and stiffened the organization of the society ; and the conflict with heresy made orthodoxy more dogmatic and intolerant. The Dark Ages were really dark ; the Church could only try to make them a little less dark than centuries of unredeemed barbarism would have made them without this witness. The Renaissance almost paganized Italy, and caused a revolt among the northern nations. The Counter-Reformation left the

Western Church Latin, not Catholic, and the Protestant Churches have split up into sects. The only true apostolic succession has been in the lives of the saints. Christianity has at least as much reason as Palestinian Judaism to beware of the traditions of the elders. Error does not become more respectable by being petrified.

We must go back to our Lord's own teaching for our real authority. But, unhappily, modern criticism has made this appeal very difficult. There are many who think that the historical Jesus has been buried under a mass of hortatory and apologetic literature, first in the form of Christianized Messianism and then of Hellenistic philosophy. The attempts to modernize our Lord, and make His teaching and character normative for civilizations utterly unlike the society in which He lived when on earth, have been severely dealt with by the latest critics of the Gospel sources. Some of them, as I have said, treat the historical Jesus as a rather obscure prophet with a purely " eschatological " message. If this were true, very little of permanent value can be found in His teaching ; His connection with the great society which bears His name becomes almost accidental. I have argued, in this volume, against a theory which would tear up historical Christianity by the roots.

I think that a clear outline of universal ethics can be found in the Gospels as they stand, and that certain principles of inexhaustible value can be drawn from these records, even if we have to admit numerous accretions which are due to the apostolic Church and not to the Founder Himself. I emphasized the law of inwardness—"from within, out of the heart of man";—the supremacy of love over justice; the law of gain through pain, of victory through sacrifice; the indignation of Christ towards three things—hypocrisy, hard-heartedness, and worldliness; the new virtues for which the Church needed new names—love, joy, humility, faith, and hope. These, I think, constitute a definite moral ideal, based on a definite standard of values, which had never been so clearly taught before.

The Gospel was a message of spiritual redemption, not of social reform. To suppose that if Christ came to earth again He would be a political agitator is to misunderstand completely His estimate of the things that really matter. And His doctrine that both good and evil proceed from the heart of the individual is flatly opposed to the ideas of Rousseau, Marx, and the revolution generally. The Bolsheviks hate Christianity not because they do not understand it, but because they do.

I have dealt shortly with the current criticisms of Christian morality, which I think are easily answered. But I have admitted that the New Testament shows a strange blindness about the future of mankind on this earth. We must make allowance for the Messianic dream, and apply the principles of the Gospel to conditions which never came within the purview of Christ's little flock.

Two aberrations seemed to call for detailed treatment. Asceticism invaded and captured the Church from without. In some of its manifestations it is insane and repulsive. But we must be careful not to burn the wheat with the chaff. It is the duty of every Christian to keep himself in fairly hard training ; and if a few feel that they are called to " forsake all " in their quest for the pearl of great price, it is not for us to say that they have chosen badly. Our civilization is too complicated ; a rigid simplification of life would be good for many of us in every way. In fact, as I have said, it is easier to fall below the " mistake of asceticism " than to rise above it.

I will not summarize my next chapter, on " Theocratic Imperialism." It is my conviction that on the institutional side the Church of Rome is, as Creighton said, " not a Church at all but a State in its organization, and the worst kind of State, an autocracy." The influence of fanatical institutionalism upon morals has been far-reaching, and in my judgment wholly mischievous. This should not prevent us from recognizing that historical circumstances made the rise of such a corporation inevitable, and that in the early Middle Ages the Roman Church did more good than harm.

The second half of the book is devoted to modern ethical problems, social and individual. I thought it right to call attention to the greater regard for veracity and intellectual honesty which we owe to this scientific age. Even in political and religious controversy some measure of decency is now generally observed. The scientific worker, as I have pointed out more than once, has devoted himself to the disinterested service of one of the absolute values—Truth. Such a one, whatever conclusions he may arrive at, cannot be far from the Kingdom of God. I like von Hügel's saying that science is the purgatory of religion. He means that it cleanses religion from many unworthy beliefs about God, man, and the world.

In discussing the relation of Christianity to social questions, I noticed the rather close association of Calvinism with modern industrialism, and tried to account for it. Industry in some honest calling was to take the place of the mortifications enjoined by Catholicism; the Calvinist was an ascetic of a new kind. Unfortunately, the newer type of capitalist has often appropriated a fortune rather than earned it, and is far from being an ascetic either of the Calvinistic or of the Catholic type. Nor is the deterioration confined to the rich. I quoted from an American book the most amazing figures as to the waste in America (before the slump) on various frivolities and amusements. For instance, " the boxing *industry* is reaching gigantic proportions. Mr. Dempsey received 750,000 dollars for thirty minutes' *work*, Mr. Tunney 450,000." To keep the balance true, I gave some figures for our own country in 1929. Drink, £288,800,000; bread, £80,000,000; hospitals £14,000,000; League of Nations, £115,500.

After a long discussion of the population question, of which I have already said something here, I spoke of humanitarianism, including our new indignation at cruelty to animals. I am no friend of unbalanced sentimentality, and have no objection either to capital punishment, which I should like to see deprived of its humiliating accessories and then extended to all incorrigibly anti-social offenders, nor to the time-honoured prerogatives of Orbilius the schoolmaster.

It is a commonplace that we have become much more humane since the eighteenth century. But has there not been a serious setback, which every moralist must think disquieting? There were few atrocities in the Napoleonic wars, except in the guerilla fighting in Spain. Gladstone could count on arousing public indignation by describing the cruelties of the Turks in the Balkans. But in the war between Russia and Japan the barbarous practice of leaving the wounded on the ground between the lines had already begun. The Germans at the very beginning of the Great War shot civilians to excite terror. (I know they denied this, but the evidence is conclusive in Belgium, and I have read first-hand evidence of similar conduct on the eastern front.) It is even more surprising that the unparalleled horrors which have been perpetrated by the Bolsheviks, not only in the three years when they were consolidating their reign of terror but ever since, have awakened no indignation among the masses in this country. Our countrymen were horrified by the execution of Marie Antoinette; the cold-blooded murder of the Tsar's four beautiful daughters was taken very quietly. I cannot altogether account for this change; we must regretfully admit that revulsion against cruelty, though it is normally

very strong in Great Britain, is easily dulled by
familiarity.

I discussed the scourge of war, but without
making any very practical suggestions as to how
the world can be delivered from it. Mr. Wells
and others think that patriotism is the enemy;
it should be replaced by cosmopolitanism. But
patriotism is a noble emotion, far more respectable, since it is based on love, than the class-war,
which is based on hatred. " Militarism," I said,
" has dug its own grave. There is a chance of
making patriotism what it should be, a strong
sentiment like the loyalty which a man feels for
his old school or his native town, a spirit of
emulation purged of rancour and jealousy, a
part of the poetry of life." Those who cannot
feel loyalty to such a country as ours are not to be
envied; and they are not likely to be good
Christians. But pacifist orators should remember that the main cause of modern wars is simply
fear, and that this fear is too often well justified.

In my next chapter, on personal ethics, I have
said a good word for the public school ideal, the
character of a gentleman. This has been the
fine flower of our English culture; it is recognized as such all over the world, and it is far
too good to lose. The best English Christian is
the best Englishman; we must develop and

purify the national character, not try to alter it. I am strongly in favour of national Churches. The idea of a universal Church is as obsolete and chimerical as that of a universal Empire, which is its counterpart.

I have given a good deal of space to problems of sex. We often hear that this is the last ditch, in which Christianity will die. In these questions I find myself on the side of the Puritans. The glorification of adultery in fiction, and in the practice of the idle rich and in Bohemian circles, seems to me disgusting. " It seems (I said) to be overlooked that the average man, when he has pledged himself in honour and conscience to keep a very solemn contract, does not feel at liberty to break it, and that when this promise has been made to the woman who has entrusted her life and happiness to his keeping, he does not, if he is a decent person, feel any inclination to break it."

The notion that the obligation of purity is an invention of Christian ascetics is easily disproved. I quoted a long passage from Plato, parts of which might have been written by St. Paul. For the Christian moralist, the obligation rests on the belief that to desecrate the sacraments of wedded love is degrading, and is punished by the withdrawal of the Holy Spirit from our hearts. The Church has a very hard battle in inculcating this view, which is combated by many psychologists and most psycho-analysts. But it must be maintained, though the unforgivingness of Victorian society to those who had sinned against it was hard and unchristian. A new danger has arisen in the great increase of homosexual vice, which is palliated in some quarters as a disease for which those who practise it are not responsible. This view, though it is held by medical psychologists who have written on the subject, is true, in my opinion, only in a small minority of cases. Most men who yield to this terrible temptation are psychically normal, though they may lose the power of self-control.

I cannot quite make up my mind about extending legal facilities for divorce. The subject bristles with difficulties. But I think that when a home has been broken up by the treachery of husband or wife, the erring partner and his or her paramour ought not to be whitewashed even by the law, still less by society.

In the preface of my book on Christian Ethics I said " it is probably the last considerable work that I shall have time to write," an announcement which many of my friends were good enough to regret. I was not thinking of approaching death, for as far as I know all my vital

organs are sound ; what I really meant was that
I felt that I had said my say and given my message,
and that I did not wish to become a bore. I
did not keep my resolution ; for I was invited
to give a series of addresses to the Cambridge
undergraduates, and also to give the Warburton
Lectures at Lincoln's Inn. The Warburton
Lectures were only the nucleus of a large book,
and, alas, I found while writing it that my hand
has really lost its cunning. I used to be compli-
mented on the " frosty brilliance " of my style.
The style of my last effort is neither frosty nor
brilliant ; and I spent two most exasperating
days in cutting out sentences and paragraphs in
which I had repeated myself. My kind French
critic, the Abbé Nédoncelle, who in his *La
Philosophie Religieuse en Grande Bretagne*, gives a
whole chapter to " *Le Platonisme chrétien du Doyen
Inge* "—a most careful, appreciative, and just
résumé of my life's work—says of my last book,
*rien de bien nouveau dans ces pages, pour qui a lu ses
ouvrages antérieurs ; mais un plaidoyer attachant pour
la transcendance de Dieu, et un bel effort de synthese.
Rien de nouveau?* It is what I knew myself ;
my literary work is done. After all, I had
nothing else to expect. It is quite exceptional
for a man of letters to remain at his best after
seventy. To mention two only of the greatest

names : Plato, when he wrote the *Laws*, was still a wise teacher, but he was a great writer no longer. The charm of his earlier dialogues has vanished. And Wordsworth had given his message to the world before 1820, when he had still thirty years to live. The mass of poetry which he wrote after that date would never have gained him immortality.

But though *God and the Astronomers* is not very well written, it embodies my most mature convictions on the central doctrines of theology. The question is really between theism and pantheism. Is God transcendent as well as immanent? Is His Being bound up with the existence and destiny of the creation? Is the universe the product of His power, will, and love, or is it the external aspect of His essential nature? If the universe ceased to be, would God also pass out of reality ; and if it became inert and dead, would the life of God also come to an end?

Modern philosophy, if it finds room for a God at all, tends to regard His Being as bound up with that of the universe. Even a religious thinker like Pringle Pattison is definitely committed to this view. On the other hand, what I have called the great tradition in Christian philosophy, which on this as on most other points owes much to Plato and his school, regards the visible universe as having only a derivative, sacramental, and imperfect value and existence. Coleridge said epigrammatically that whereas for Spinoza God minus the world equals nought, for Christianity " G minus W equals G." I quoted the dying words of Emily Brontë :

> Though earth and man were gone,
> And suns and universes cease to be,
> And Thou wert left alone,
> Every existence would exist in Thee.

The relation between God and the world is not a relation between two reciprocally interdependent realities, nor between two aspects of a single life in time.

The question is far from being merely speculative. The theist believes that God is eternal and unchanging, and that He has revealed Himself to man as the source of all that for our minds has unconditional and absolute value—perfect goodness, perfect truth, and perfect beauty. These are not merely ideals which we set before ourselves. They are realized in the eternal or spiritual world which the Platonists called the *cosmos noëtos*, and which Christians call heaven. It is our privilege, even while we live here, to ascend in heart and mind to this higher sphere, for it is our heart's true home, in which, as St. Paul says, we have our " conversation " or citizenship. In this better world we have our liberation from the changes and chances of our mortal life ; in this better world we find our immortality, which is something much more than endless survival in time. Philosophers and saints express this faith in their own language. Socrates claims his citizenship, not of Athens, but of the city of which the type is laid up in heaven. St. Paul says that though our earthly tabernacle be dissolved, we have a house not made with hands, eternal in the heavens. The God of pantheism offers us no such refuge. He is not safe Himself.

The loss of this eternal background has been very precariously supplied in modern times by the idea of progress, the secular faith of the nine-teenth century. It was one of my objects in writing this book to inquire whether the facts, so far as they are known to us, justify this optimism. The cruel experiences of the last twenty years have shattered our confidence that man in each generation is better and happier than he was in the time of his parents. Even the modified optimism or meliorism expressed by the saying that progress is in a spiral, not in a straight line, seems now difficult to maintain.

We have no wish to go back to barbarism; but there have been long and discouraging reversions in the history of civilization, and we cannot be confident that there will be no more of them. A dispassionate survey of history may lead us to a very chastened hopefulness, but not to any dreams of a millennium. The future, says Anatole France, is a convenient place in which to store our dreams.

But I called special attention to the opinions of men of science on the inevitable doom of the universe. I discussed, so far as my limited knowledge of science allowed me, the view, held by our leading astronomers and physicists, that the whole universe is slowly running down like a clock, and the attempts which are made to find an escape from so unwelcome and irrational a conclusion. I pointed out that the Christian tradition has always led us to expect the destruction of the world, but only as the preliminary to a better state, usually pictured as itself within the time-series. The philosophical notion of eternity does not need this latter expectation; but the picture of God, at some distant period, reigning over a dead universe is not easy to believe in. In any case, the pantheistic idea of a God Who is Himself evolving in His creation seems, as I argued, to be incompatible with the laws of nature as they are now believed to be. Either God " sitteth above the waterflood and remaineth a King for ever," or, as the mere *anima mundi*, He is less than divine, for the universe is under sentence of death.

This led me to a consideration of the status of time in reality, one of the most difficult problems in philosophy. Here I found myself in substantial agreement with the main tradition of Catholic philosophy, and in opposition to writers like Bergson, Croce, and some well-known English writers. Some of my critics were surprised at my friendly attitude towards Romanist thinkers, since my dislike of institutional Catholicism was well known. But there was no inconsistency. I have learnt much from Baron von Hügel, and I admire the lucidity and clear thinking of the neo-Thomist school. My only serious difference from them is in their dualism of the natural and the supernatural. Even the most Liberal Catholics seem unable to see the objections to a theory which intercalates acts of God into the order of nature. But this is not my subject in the book of which I am speaking.

In the spring of 1933 I was asked to take part in a kind of " mission " (this word was wisely avoided) to Cambridge undergraduates. I had given a course in St. Paul's the year before for the young people of London; the response was most encouraging. I have for several years preached a university sermon at Cambridge, and have certainly succeeded in getting the ear of the younger members of the university. The addresses, which I gave in February 1933, were very well attended. I published them under the title of *Things New and Old*. They contain, I think, most of what I wished to say to the rising generation, who are facing fairly cheerfully what to their elders seems a not very cheerful prospect. My main thesis is that we must build on the old foundation, but fully recognizing that there are new problems which cannot be solved by relying on tradition. A general overturn is not what is wanted; but there must be a courageous adaptation of fundamental Christian principles to new conditions, and a readiness to accept new discoveries as a divine revelation, the message of the Spirit to our time.

I did not think it fair that I should continue to hold the Deanery of St. Paul's, to which I had been appointed solely as a minor prophet, after, in my own judgment, I had given my message, as well as I could, to my generation. And so I determined to send in my resignation in the autumn of 1934, soon after my seventy-fourth birthday. When I had once made up my mind that this was the right thing to do, I was not troubled by doubts or regrets. I loved my beautiful official residence; and I loved my circle of friends, in whom I was very fortunate. My position brought us into contact with some of the most interesting personalities of our time. We enjoyed the friendship of Lord Haldane, to whose immense public services his countrymen did only tardy justice. Almost every year we stayed at Cloan in the summer, and became intimate with other members of a gifted family. Lord and Lady Burghclere invited us every year to the houses in Scotland which they took in the summer; and after the death of Lord Burghclere we saw a great deal of Lady Burghclere and her sisters, who have been the kindest of friends to us. Among other great friends are Sir Lawrence and Lady Jones, and Mrs. Carruthers (Violet Markham). Lady Horner and Mrs. Knatchbull in Somersetshire have been most cordial and hospitable. Among prominent churchmen we received much kindness from Archbishop Davidson, though I am afraid I made him uneasy at times, and from the Bishop of Durham, the most loyal and affectionate of friends. These are only a few names among many which we shall always remember with affection and gratitude. Some of our friendships I hope we may keep: but of course we owed them to the position which I have just quitted. The Dean of St. Paul's is also brought into close connection with the Mansion House and the City Companies. This again was a part of my duties or privileges which I greatly enjoyed. And I always looked forward with keen pleasure to the meetings of my two dining-clubs, the oddly-named "Nobody's Friends," which was founded by a small group of men including Joshua Watson, and his brother Archdeacon Watson, my great-grandfather; and "The Brotherhood," a small clerical society, the members of which all enjoy each other's company.

Sed haec prius fuere. I am now on the shelf, or rather I shall be when this little book, which my publisher has asked me to write in the summer of 1934, sees the light. What ought one to feel, and what do I actually feel, in entering upon the last lap of my race? The dismal chapter of Ecclesiastes about old age has a trembling fascination for the young; but the old can face the facts more genially, like the poet Collins.

" And when I at last must throw off this frail covering
 Which I've worn for threescore years and ten,
On the brink of the grave I'll not seek to keep
   hovering,
  Nor my thread wish to spin o'er again :

But my face in the glass I'll serenely survey,
　And with smiles count each wrinkle and furrow ;
As this old worn-out stuff which is threadbare to-day
　May become everlasting to-morrow."

I cannot make my own the opinion of Browning's
Rabbi ben Ezra, that old age is the best time of
life ; but still less can I agree with the Greek
poets who prayed that they might die at sixty.
(No doubt in ancient Greece the aged, with no
spectacles or false teeth, had a poor time of it.)
The good man, says Sir Thomas Overbury
bravely, feels old age rather by the strength of
his soul than by the weakness of his body.
" Though our outward man perish, yet our
inward man is renewed day by day." We have
all seen this in the lives of good old people whom
we have known. We do not look to them,
perhaps, for new ideas ; but they have the
strength that resides in quietness and confidence,
and they may often comfort the young, who
have received some knock-down blow, since
they have learned that time heals almost all
wounds. Some blemishes which were discern-
ible in middle life are refined away when ambition
and anxiety no longer disturb the mind. The
character of an old man sometimes acquires a
distinction which it wanted before.

Every age has its own proper characteristics,

which we should not wish either to anticipate or to prolong. The rich colours of autumn are as beautiful and right and natural as the delicate greens of spring ; they are not only the signs of decay, the harbingers of death. " Go thou thy way till the end be, for thou shalt rest and stand in thy lot at the end of the days." This promise to Daniel is God's word to the Christian soul when night is closing in. Rest and be calm. Leave to others the whirl and bustle of life. If God sends comfort, thank Him. If He sends loneliness and suffering, still thank Him ; we are being detached from this world to prepare us, we hope, for a better. I think, as we grew old, we realize more and more the truth of Lewis Nettleship's words in a letter to a friend, " Death does not count."

And yet no one who has taken a keen interest in the changes which have come to human society in the troubled period through which it has been his lot to live can help looking forward as well as back, not for himself, but for his friends, his country, and his Church. There is a strong tendency to hope that the causes in which we believe are on the way to triumph. Perhaps there is an element of make-believe in this, as when we spurn away the old year as a guest who has overstayed his welcome, and greet the new year with smiles which are not likely to last long. But no pure hope shall wither, except that a purer may spring out of its roots. If it is our lot to " die in faith, not having received the promise "—and this is the lot of all who have worked for humanity, " some better thing," probably very unlike what we hoped for, may be in store for those who come after us. We may hope this without deluding ourselves with the dream of an inevitable " law of progress."

The Great War has not only speeded up several changes which were coming about slowly and gradually before it broke out. It has knocked the bottom out of some articles of faith which were very confidently proclaimed fifty or sixty years ago. When I was young, there was still a robust complacency about the course which events were taking. " Our glorious constitution." " The empire on which the sun never sets." " The irresistible tide of liberty and democracy." " Trust the people." Who does not remember (if he was then alive) these and other catchwords of a fat and comfortable generation ? Science was proclaiming, with what now seems incredible shallowness, that the " riddle of the universe " had been solved. In religion, " the power not ourselves that makes for righteousness " was displacing the anthropomorphic God of the Bible. How simple it all was ; and how satisfactory to find that Herbert Spencer really knew a great deal about " the Unknowable " ! The positive existence of a transcendent Absolute, he tells us, is " a necessary datum of consciousness. The belief which this datum constitutes has a higher warrant than any other whatever." After all, there was not much difference between the champion of agnosticism and St. Thomas Aquinas ! And in morals I was delighted to find the positivist Frederic Harrison exclaiming indignantly, " A man who cannot control his appetites is a cad. There is no real love except in marriage." The nineteenth century never carried its theories to their logical conclusions. When we consider how unsound its theories often were, it was well for those who held them that they knew when to trust to their healthy instincts.

The whole edifice of nineteenth-century Liberalism now seems to be in ruins. The Great War has made the world permanently *unsafe* for democracy. None of our institutions, certainly not the Church, has lost in prestige anything like so much as the House of Commons. In the few countries where popular government still survives, the elected governors are either despised or hated, or both. We cannot any

longer worship the fetish of democracy; we
have seen it at too close quarters. It did its
work, mainly destructive, in clearing away the
relics of feudalism, privilege, and snobbishness;
it educated the nation, up to a point, but we have
had to learn that power, in the hands of the many
as of the few, is never used well.

The history of Europe since the Middle Ages
has been a record of *emancipation*. Kings, priests,
independent parliaments, traditional dogmas, and
ethical principles, have been dethroned one after
the other; and now a sharp reaction has come.
The nations are beginning to cry, not only
"Down with democracy," but "Down with
liberty." Did any wise people, fifty years ago,
see that this was coming? Herbert Spencer,
perhaps, was an exception; but I confess that I
did not realize so early that the giant Democracy
had feet of clay.

The driving force of the socialistic movement
has hitherto been the acquisitiveness and materialism which the working class learned from those
who called themselves their betters. There was
in fact no rational or moral justification for the
plutocracy of Queen Victoria's reign. The
territorial magnates of earlier generations really
governed the country, and if they lived in com-
fortless magnificence in dark, draughty, and

insanitary palaces, there was a long feudal tradition behind them. But there is no reason why a successful brewer or tobacconist should ape the style of a grand seigneur. Now, however, the "workers" have nothing to gain and much to lose by upsetting the social order. Their incomes, when we add to them their exemptions from taxation and all that they draw from the public purse, are about the average family incomes for the whole country; and the few large fortunes which still exist would be very easy to destroy and very difficult to distribute. Unskilled labour is now almost as well paid as skilled. The dole has put a weapon into the hand of the unskilled workman. We may hope therefore that the class war may gradually become a thing of the past, though unhappily when the fathers have eaten sour (or too many sweet) grapes, the children's teeth will be set on edge.

There is, however, an intellectual socialism, or rather half a dozen incompatible schemes which are much in the air just now. The words "rationalization," "planning," "organization," are in everyone's mouth. Whether government officials would be likely to plan and organize intelligently is seldom asked; their record hitherto does not inspire confidence. My own opinion is that the only socialism which could be made to work is Russian state-capitalism, miscalled communism ; and that the price which would have to be paid, the total destruction of liberty, the placing of the life, livelihood, and liberty of every man, and the honour of every woman, at the absolute disposal of State commissars, is far too high a price for the efficiency of a cast-iron bureaucracy. It is quite certain that our people would never stand it ; and therefore I think that, following our invariable practice hitherto in this country, we shall try to mend our existing institutions, and not destroy them.

The most pressing problem is no longer that of reducing economic inequalities, but of removing the anxiety and insecurity which harass almost all sections of the population. The prevailing unemployment, which is now endemic, is probably the effect of several causes—over-population; the loss of our foreign trade; the rapid and progressive increase in labour-saving contrivances, which in some trades enable one man to do the work of twenty; and the employment of women as wage-earners.[1] No remedy has yet been found. A vicious circle is thus set up. The obstacles to emigration, perhaps not insurmountable

[1] The importance of this last factor has, I think, been exaggerated. Married women in this country do not very often earn wages, and the proportion of those who do so has not increased since the War. The chief change has been the transfer of a large number of young women from domestic service to work in shops and factories.

but certainly very grave, have already been
mentioned in these pages. A reduction in
population would have to be very drastic to be
of much use, and the benefits would not be felt
for many years. And meanwhile, the demoraliza-
tion of those who have been on the dole for
many years is obvious and inevitable. But I
cannot help hoping that the evil will sooner or
later be overcome ; and if it can be, our children
may live to see a happier England, in which one
of the chief problems will be the organization of
leisure for those whose daily work will occupy
only a few hours a day, thanks to the blessings,
now not always indisputable, of applied science.

How have these changes affected the national
character ? The families which formerly were
rich or well-to-do seem to me to have accepted
the destruction of their standard of living with
great cheerfulness and public spirit. Money,
which was certainly overvalued when I was
young, is not much thought of by the rising
generation. It is impossible any longer to
" found a family," and now that the tax-collector
lies in wait for all large savings, accumulation is
not worth while. The poor investor, however,
is much more favourably situated. Between
3,000 and 4,000 million pounds have been
invested in small sums since the War. We are

becoming a nation of small rentiers, like the French, a fact which should make for political stability. I do not think that a Christian ought to regret the dethronement of Mammon. It is only since the industrial revolution that our nation has got the reputation of being over-fond of money. I think it probable that what is called rationalization in industry will go farther, and that " capital " (which is only a term of abuse for the other fellow's savings used productively) will continue to receive hard measure. But I do not expect what is usually meant by revolution in this country.

In morals, especially in the narrower sense, history shows that periods of licence and Puritanism alternate, and that a great war or social upheaval is normally followed by a relaxation of all restraints. A similar reaction may follow a régime of repressive rigorism, such as the domination of Cromwell, and, to a less extent, the repressions and taboos of Queen Victoria's reign. There has already, I think, been some return to decency after the extravagances of the post-War years. But recovery must depend on the acceptance of a nobler view of life. I think Mr. Alfred Noyes, in his beautiful new book *The Unknown God*, is justified in his complaint that the exponents of our art and literature to-day,

with few exceptions, have no belief in real values.
" They are giving over to analysis what was
meant for synthesis ; and where they should be
creative, or interpretative of life in its fullness,
they offer us dissections and the disintegrated
relics of a post-mortem." He adds severely
that many of them prefer the ugly to the beautiful,
and doubt whether lust may not be the " higher
continence," breaking your pledged word a
nobler form of freedom, and evil itself the higher
good. " Fair is foul and foul is fair. Hover
through the fog and filthy air." It is possible
that, as Mr. Noyes suggests, our pre-occupation
with the world as portrayed by natural science
may have made us think meanly of human nature,
forgetting that these marvels would have no
existence if there were no minds, human or
divine, to perceive them. The Eighth Psalm
ought to be a sufficient corrective ; but the
little-known seventeenth-century poet, Thomas
Traherne, has expressed the philosophy of
nature and mind in very beautiful lines.

> All my mind was wholly everywhere.
> Whate'er it saw, 'twas actually there ;
> The Sun, ten thousand stages off, was nigh ;
> > The utmost star
> > Tho' seen from far
> Was present in the apple of mine eye.

O wonder and delight !
O sacred mystery !
My soul a spirit wide and bright
An image of the Deity !
A most substantial light !
That being greatest which did nothing seem.

I do not attach much importance to the curious
fashion which has led about a dozen men of
letters to join the Church of Rome. Some of
them we need not be sorry to have lost ; but
there are at least two, Mr. Noyes himself and
Mr. Dawson, whose defection has caused me
real grief. It is useless to speculate on their
motives ; we can only notice that while in the
Roman Catholic countries (including, I am told,
even Southern Ireland) the Church is losing
ground steadily, without, however, causing any
compensating gain to other forms of Christianity,
in the Protestant countries, such as Great Britain,
Holland, Northern Germany, and the United
States, Romanism is gaining slightly in numbers,
and still more in prestige. Perhaps both were to
to be expected. The old rule, *cuius regio, eius
religio* was quite irrational. And in those countries where this Church has little or no secular
power, it is able to disguise the qualities which
have aroused hatred against it in the South of
Europe. The Church of England arouses no

sectarian enthusiasm, because it stands simply for the religion of the people of England. But its broad tolerance should make it ready to welcome any genuine revival of spiritual religion in this country. It certainly has a place in Christendom which no other religious body could fill.

The Liberal Protestantism which forty years ago seemed to be the natural religion for an educated man has partly lost its appeal. We are told that Harnack, the greatest theological scholar of his time, is very little read in Germany, and the same is probably true of England. The position of this school may perhaps be understood best from Harnack's brilliant course of lectures translated under the title *What is Christianity?* The author attempts, much as Sir John Seeley did in *Ecce Homo*, to disengage the vital parts of the Gospel message for the benefit of Christians in our own day, after eliminating the legendary and mythical elements from the narratives. A portrait emerges of the supreme Teacher of morals, Who in His life also was our perfect pattern. This school was at first blamed by the orthodox for presenting us with a " reduced Christianity." The picture of Christ, it was said, was both modernized and deprived of the supernatural character which even the earliest of the Gospels clearly assigns to Him. But modernist criticism complains that Harnack as a critic stops half-way. He gives a portrait of a historical figure, of which strict history knows next to nothing. This is the destructive criticism of Loisy and his followers, which, as Loisy intended, has injured Protestantism more than Catholicism, for Catholics are not allowed to read it. There is no doubt that scepticism about the value of the historical record has shaken Liberal Protestantism very seriously in Germany, and to some extent in England. Personally, I think Loisy's extreme incredulity is perverse, though I recognize that he is an extremely able critic. But I cannot rest content with Harnack's view, which shows little sympathy with the Pauline Christ-mysticism, though this was unquestionably the core of the great apostle's faith, and not much with the great tradition in Christian philosophy, which also has its roots in the New Testament.

But I must bring these discursive reflections to an end. What are the most precious gifts for which an old man, looking back on his life, ought to thank God? The Greeks put *health* first. I have never had a day's serious illness in my life, and I do not know who told M. Nédoncelle that I suffer from *une santé délicate*. But I have known so many men and women who have triumphantly overcome this handicap, that I could not rank health as the best thing in life. Some kind of recognition and encouragement is, I think, almost essential to happiness, except for a few proud or heroic natures. I have certainly had nothing to complain of under this head. But I have not the slightest doubt that domestic happiness is the greatest of all good gifts, next to that of "wisdom," for which Solomon prayed, and which I suppose, may be defined as a right judgment of the relative value of things. The blessings which God has given me in my wife and children are in a different class from all other sources of happiness and pleasure that have come to me. At a time when many persons are not ashamed to assert that marriage is generally a failure, it is permissible to give this personal testimony. And though it may be my private opinion that no one else has been quite so fortunate as myself, I shall not quarrel with the countless other happy couples who think that they have been similarly favoured.

The Greeks had a proverb : " The works of the young, the counsels of the middle-aged, the prayers of the old." Perhaps the counsels of the old, and their predictions, are not of much value. But our prayers may not be useless. These, at any rate, we may humbly offer up, with faith and hope that the God who has kept us from our youth up until now will be with our children and grandchildren on the unknown path which they must tread. For " we have not passed this way heretofore."

Printed in Great Britain by the KEMP HALL PRESS LTD.
in the City of Oxford